1-9-14

To-Olivia

Love, Peace and more Blessings

Rose

Disclaimer

This book is sold with the inner and over-standing the author and publisher are not rending medical, psychological or any professional advice. This book was written to provide information in regard to the subject matter written here.
(Do your own research)

Some names have been changed.

THE BOOK

WITHOUT A NAME

You Read It, You Name It

ROSE Whaley

Universal Truths Publishing

Bronx, New York

The Book Without A Name

Universal Truths Publishing
646-463-6369
Email: chakraspectrums@netzero.net
www.chakraspectrums.com
Cover art graphics- channeled from Spirit/Rose Whaley
ISBN: 0-9777523-0-5
"'Scripture taken from the NEW AMERICAN STANDARD BIBLE®,
©Copyright 1960, 1962, 1963, 1968, 1971, 1972, 1973, 1975, 1977
By The Lockman Foundation
Used by permission." www.Lockman.org
Metaphysical Bible Dictionary, Unity School of Christianity
Visit www.unityonline.org
Revealing Word (A Dictionary of Metaphysical Terms) by Charles Fillmore
Reference Library – Unity
Visit www.unityonline.org

New number
1 718-933-4643

Contents

To: my loving Godmother,

MAGNOLIA SALEM

In loving memory

Sunrise: April 2, 1920
Sunset: June 5, 2002 to

CLIFFORD BAILEY, who stared editing this book in 2005, He took his life in May 2005, thus, transcending out of the physical, a month before he made his transition, (died) he told me I was writing this book for him because he had a lot of mental and emotional disharmonies, saying he did found some love, peace, and some comfort in my words

Special-Thanks

To my inspirational friends and spirit guide Benji Titus and Spiritual Mother Susie Bank Williams, Dr. Reverend Eric Butterworth (from UNITY church), The Teaching of the Buddha, Dr. Joy Leary and Dr. John H. Clarke (Black historian), all of whose teachings I love and many more. Thanks for the Grace of the Creator for channeling this book cover design for this book and the empowering knowledge and wisdom.

The Revealing Word a metaphysical dictionary of terms by Charles Fillmore (Reference Library C.F. a must-have book) Metaphysical Bible Dictionary by Unity the New Scofield Study Bible and to all the many authors for their great quotes. For all the truly loving people who came out on one of the coldest day for my first and second book signing at Barns & Noble.

And last but not least, to anyone who I did not name who inspire and showed me true love, you know who you are and to the ones that did not, **all are appreciated and LOVE TOO!**

About the Author

My given name is Rosemary Williams, Whaley was my married name **(which I will be deleting)**, and I incarnated on **September 9, 1950**, in Savannah, Georgia, my parents **Lillie and Corrie Williams.** I moved to **New York at the age of twelve, dropped out of the tenth grade at Morris High School in the Bronx, New York**, and became a mother at the age of fifteen with my first child **Herman Jr. I married at sixteen** years of age, and had two more children, **Adrienne (Baby) and Clifford (Shine). I'm also the grandmother of Lesley Davis Jr., now a great grandmother. I resolved** (healed) or **dissolve** the experiences from a **dysfunctional childhood** (which rendered me a **wounded inner child)**, experience **being molested** as a young girl, **two attempted rapes, and an abusive marriage** of ten years **(resulted in me almost killing my husband).** I experienced **several suicide attempts**; I healed a so-called **incurable disease** and other **illnesses.** At one point, I was nearsighted, survived a **car accident, filed bankruptcy,** lived on welfare, had **two abortions, a miscarriage** and had a **profound revelation** that I wrote briefly about in my **1996 newletter on my website,** went for **psychotherapy for about a year, I was arrested for shoplifting** (one of many addictions). I know now I signed a **spiritual contract** before choosing to **incarnate here** at this time for **another SOUL PURPOSE. Don't compromise (SELL) YOUR SOUL.** I stop taking **FLU SHOTS over thirty years ago** and haven't had the **flu since. I no longer suffer** with **psychological back pain. I have transmuted my lower vibration to a higher consciousness where the healing already exists.**

I am first a child of the Creator; I am a self-taught designer/seamstress since 1968. I opened my first custom-made clothing boutique in 1978 on 149th Street and the second in 1994 on Fordham Road, both in the Bronx. My fashions have been featured in several magazines, as well as the Daily News, on cable TV shows, at the Apollo Theatre, The cotton club in Harlem N. Y. in Guyana, South America, at many colleges, and at New Life and Kwanzaa expos. I received certificates in business, modeling, and a course in herbology from the Birth Choices Center in Brooklyn. I have three different trademarks: Mind Over Body Fashion Connection, Conscious People Choice's and The Seven Chakra Spectrum for apparel, toys, paper goods, glassware, and linens. I am the producer of my cable TV show entitled, "Self- Awareness: Whom Truth?" Over a two year period, I produced a series of newsletters (since 2001), and facilitate my free self-awareness workshops in Manhattan and for the YMC-Bisexual N-transgender community- Moon Fire, for residents of a Norwalk, Connecticut, halfway house for male offenders serving out their remaining sentences, and for various other groups.

I had an out-of-body experience in 1987 and have had many more visions, both personal and universal. I have been teaching spirituality, metaphysics, and counseling people of all races, ages, and cultural backgrounds for many years, helping people to help themselves and re-discover their TRUTH. I have talked people out of thinking they wanted to end their lives, because they, like myself, thought it was the way to escape the pain they couldn't suppress, hide, run from, or cover up, not knowing that the way was getting the right help and going within to heal and release painful emotions. My challenges was to learn how to depend on and trust the Goddess I am, to recognize my own inner power, and how to apply it correctly for the good of all humanity in order to remember my soul mission for being here. I am now learning to develop the healing energies in my hands in order to practice what is called the **"laying on of hands."** Not knowing what I was doing I used this technique on my mother when she had an **aneurysm** and during a **seminar** when a participant **was** having a seizure in the Gay community.

Her true spirit told she is a teacher, not a preacher. Like **Mahatma Gandhi** said, **"My life is my message."** You are the Master Builder of your life. The Creator gave you everything you need; learn to believe and trust in your **Goddesses and Gods! Know what God wants you to do and do it without becoming corrupt, and selling your SOUL!**

Some people are successful in spite of the obstacles by facing them. Without compromising or selling their souls, without saying or doing deceitful, disingenuous things that are belittling to themselves, their race, and to humanity for the sake of riches, people want material things that in the end has **no real value.** It's all an illusion for those who don't know their **authentic self. There is nothing greater than you! Life** is about **God consciousness, balance, and you!**

What characterizes a really great person with TRUE INTEGRITY and the COURAGE to STAND-UP for his or her CONVICTIONS, NO MATTER WHAT? Such great people are Malcolm X, Mother Theresa, Clara Hale (Hale House), Muhammad Ali (for standing up against the Vietnam War), Fannie Lou Hamer, Nelson Mandela, Dr. Lorraine Day (a self-healed cancer survivor who spoke out against the medical system), Vernon Johnson (a civil rights activist who paved the way for Martin Luther King, Jr.), Jack Johnson (a boxer who wouldn't conform to this bogus system), James Brown (the singer who sang I'm Black & I'm Proud that did inspired some people of color. Adam Clayton Powell Jr., Gil Noble (talk show host of Like It Is), Bob Marley (Get up Stand Up), India Arie many songs, John Lennon (Imagine), and KRS-One (Higher Level), many positive songs/singers. Dr. Catherine Hamlin (who is medically assisting women in Africa as broadcasted on Oprah), The Tuskegee Airmen, Book: BLACK LIES WHITE LIES Truth according to TONY BROWN-Conspiracy that is stealing your MONEY, Michael Moore for showing truths in his documentary movies and many more movies, pay attention to the true message.

"A person with true wisdom is more valuable and wealthy than a person with riches, fame, and a limited education." -Rose Whaley

"A false balance is an abomination to the Lord, but a just weight is his delight. When false pride comes, then come dishonor, but with the humble is wisdom. The integrity of the upright will guide them, but the falseness of the treacherous will destroy them. Riches do not profit in the day of wrath, but righteousness of the blameless will smooth his way. But righteousness of the upright will deliver them. But the treacherous will be caught by theirs own greed." -Proverb 11:1-6

Rose's studies and inner and over-standing have taught her that her ruling energy planet is Mars since she was born (incarnated) in September (on the ninth day), she have a lot of warrior energy and a strong sense of purpose. She interested in the studying of the cosmos now more than ever.

THE WORST THING AN AWAKEN PERSON CAN DO, IS NOTHING TO HELP WAKE-UP HUMANITY.

Rose's vision (Divine Mission/ Contract) is to manifest the Self-Awareness Center for all humanity; to help remind people of who they really are; to remind individuals not to be totally co-dependent on anyone or anything other than their Goddess/Godself; to tap into their divine power within to create the life they truly deserve (which is our birth right); to help people help themselves spiritually; and to provide housing for some that are experiencing a temporary transition. It's already done in Spirit! She learned how to live in a consciousness of DIVINE GRACE, PRAYER, GRATITUBE, and DIVINE LOVE EVERYDAY!

Clip on youtube-2014 Sun Son activation with Story waters AKA the meaning...

Danny Searle-What happen when or if we don't ascend and Bashar-Go with the flow or get left behind.

"There are no unnatural or supernatural phenomena, only very big gaps in our knowledge of what is natural. We should strive to fill those gaps of ignorance."
-Edgar D. Mitchell

"The Goddess/God in Me Greets the Goddess/God in You."
All Love offering (ENERGY EXCHANGE) are Appreciated! Would you help us!

Introduction

WORDS TO THE WISE! The KEY is in your HEART! That sparks
of pure light (THE SOUL) PURSUIT YOUR TRUE SELF!

AQUARIUS AGE this is a magnificent time, filled with new
opportunity (do you research).This book was not written with the
intention to make Rose rich or famous. this is simply her evolving
spiritual journey with enriching experiences, written with a sincere
intention to help others learn (remember) inner and over-stand to grow,
and remember who they truly are to raise their frequency to heal, and
realize theirs truth and evolve, back to Goddesses and Gods and re-
claim their divine power. This book was channeled through her from
the TRUE SUPREME CREATOR to share with anyone who has an
open mind, heart and a teachable Spirit. Most people are afraid to
wake-up to truth, self-reflection and change, unwilling to listen, afraid of
critical thinking, true meditation and deep researching on their own,
stepping out of their comfort zone of conformity. The majority of the
population seems content with regurgitating what has been conditioned
and programmed in their minds as their own thoughts and beliefs.
Learning and inner and over-standing your divine lessons from your
experience is your best teacher. She uses the word "inner/over
and standing" in this book to represent a higher knowing
exceeding a human manufactured level of doubt,
misunderstanding, confusion and misinterpreted.

Rose is not writing this book to convert, convince, manipulate, seduce,
condition, or program (enslave) anyone mind to believe, accept, or
conform to any organized group, or person or church. Her heart goes
out to the majority of people coerced by false government and the
main media and passed down religious misleading propaganda. They
don't realize that this has been done to them! Her story is written to

initiate thought-provoking questions, deep research and provide inspiration and divine techniques for those seeking to remember their ENLIGHTENMENT Creator Truth! Not men false truth for mind control and greed.

These are some of Rose's spiritual realization, that our true Spirit is forever perfect, complete, and whole and does not know limitation, illnesses, pains or physical hindrances. We perpetuate conditions into a place of discord and imbalance that are programmed in our unconscious mind; we learned to settle for a hypnotic state of being. Our lives are adversely impacted by varying degrees of distress predicated on our level of education, all relationships, parenting skills, religious involvement, materialism and environmental stimulus. Our subconscious minds always accept what is constantly seen, felt, or heard without discerning between good or bad. We erroneously convince ourselves that what we see, feel, and hear is good and feels right; therefore, it must be GOD'S WILL (Read Romans 14:11-14).

Our psychic abilities /intuition /sixth sense is a gift from Creator, which is shut down at an early age which is replaced with only a formal, limited mis- education instead of true knowledge and wisdom of who you truly are and your soul purpose. The influx of radio, television, telephone, computers, fashions, entertainment, sports, cosmetic surgery, false politicians, religious and spiritual leaders have caused us to search outside ourselves for our self-worth. What kind of system makes celebrities, athletes, politicians, and preachers more valued and higher paid than good school teachers, healthcare and sanitation workers, policemen, firemen (risk their life), and soldiers who go to war for this country's bogus lies (she have personally experienced the loss of a beloved brother, killed at nineteen in the Vietnam War after being drafted (FORCED) at the (tender age of eighteen.) The problem is most people don't know who the real so call enemies are and we don't fix the cause; we just focus on the affect not the cause. She couldn't understand how we are so willing to sacrifice our most valuable asset - DIVINE spirits! Back in the 1960's, Edwin Starr song says "War! "What is it good for?" Truly, it's only good for their (?) hidden agendas. Read the excerpt "How to Stop Terrorism? Stop Being Terrorists!" from Michael Moore book, Dude, Where's My Country? Stop believing ideology of mind control. Be aware but don't give your Divine Power to anyone.

Are you truly ready to change any aspect of your life for the greater reality? Are you ready for true self-discovery? Are you ready for the inner and over-standing to express your true feelings in order to reconnect to CREATOR/ GOD CONSCIOUSNESS? Are you ready to tap into more of your divine power, wisdom, courage, wealth, health, compassion, peace, and joy? Are you ready to live fearless to resolve obstacles and experience unconditional love and wholeness with the universe? Everything vibrates in a pattern of perfection that existed long before we were created. Distortions in our energy field or grid work are at the heart of all states of disease and disharmony (problems). True knowledge of our subtle natures is the key to inner and over-standing the process that engenders universe balance feminine and masculine energy. Not Over-standing circumvents succumbing to addictions or activities outside of your true self, such as joining small or large malicious groups regulated by ignorance, hate and fear (e.g., Ku Klux Klan, Nazi Party), false religions that deny the existence of your true Goddess/God self-residing within you and our consciousness is kept stuck in a low frequency with altered foods, detrimental music and television programs, excessive sports participation, obsessive celebrity idolization, Solely relying on the Bible content which was re- edited many time by many difference people, some books completely deleted and in most cases misinterpreted. Worshipping of the physical and material things, etc...things that distract you from your true self and true power (John 4:24). Until we center ourselves in our true essence, we will never resolve or dissolve our addictions or the replacement of one addiction with another unconsciously. Our innate craving for wholeness is of a transcendental nature, greater than the physical self and cannot be placated by our addictions and mindless quests for only physical pleasure. Unfortunately we continue to seek our spiritual salvation from institutions and individuals that are themselves UN-awaken spiritually or UN-PURE HEART. The inner self seeks to rediscover the true meaning of our spirit and soul. Our true power of self is designed to give re- birth to the "God" embryo within us waiting to be reborn. To live a free, joyous, and a fully creative life, we must lose our fear of inferiority. Your life journey is not about "MAN" and the "Church" or anything else. It's about "The Creator" and the Goddess/God in YOU!

In March of 1987, Rose was diagnosed with a (so-called) incurable disease named Sarcoidosis. It was then that she recognized the true voice of God louder than man's. The fear and possibility of prolonged suffering and dying really woke her up to a reality she thought was unknown to her. She had to be willing to give up who she had become like, feeling fearful, powerless, inferior and ignorant of her true self to become whom Spirit created her to be: fearless, powerful, aware, loving a Co- Creator (Godlike). Rose asked and it was given; she sought and found; she knocked and the door was open. (Read Matthew 7:7). She consciously set out to seek a cure; as a result she found the key and let herself out of her CAGE, and reconnected to her True Goddess Self within her HEART and SOUL.

"He/she who comes to know him/herself knows all things."
-Anonymous

The moment Rose was able to see clearly, and listen to only the still small voice of Yahweh, Eloheem (God) her/his truth, her healing began.

Knowing the difference between God's truth and man's lies allows her to live in peace, love, courage, and without false guilt, obligation, inferiority and fears. Being in tune she learned self-acceptance and gratitude, Rose have grown exponentially from all of her so call bad, painful experiences, inner and over-standing the healing principle of the Creator, knowing how and why she created all the pain, illness, financial and relationships problems. She healed the dis-ease by tapping into the healing energy that are always present, growing and ridding herself of all ailments, including: migraines, allergies, gastritis, female problems, hiatus hernia, hemorrhoid, arthritic lower back pain, tonsillitis, varicose veins, muscle spasms, sinus problems, and heartburn and many more imbalances. And gaining control of her mind and spirit, inner/over-standing and applying universal laws, Rose started realizing the mind is a tremendous atom-splitting cyclotron ready to release a stream of dynamic creative energy at any moment. She knows the mind will form an outer reality from whatever we feel and imprint in our UN or SUB- CONSCIOUS MIND. She recognized that God is a force like invisible electro-magnetic energy, and the same is true of our bodies; we can learn to generate our magnetism to attract what we really deserve and in divine order.

In 1987, Rose had an out-of-body experience and re- discovered for herself that there is a world greater and a divine plan, than this physical one and all divine spirits are Co-Creators of this power and are all ONE. She started having clearer and more frequent visions, such as the 9-11 World Trade Center experience six years before it happened, a deadly plague, catastrophic earth- quake yet to hit New York City, a Tsunami whether it's natural or man-made (haarp).(RESEARCH)

Rose is now instructed by faith with trust, instead of fear, guilt, false obligation, ignorance and attachments. She followed her true Spirit stepping out of her comfort zone, into a new adventure of divine reality. It leads her to places where she interacted with spiritual (not religious) people of all different cultures. She never heard of or thought of going to **meditation groups, spiritual lectures, seminars, or retreats.** Earlier in her life she believed religion and spirituality were one and the same. **Since her initial journey of awakening (remembering),** she now knows that the two principles are distinctly different. **Spirituality is about knowing divine truth and our powerful God/Goddess self** and the importance of its presence in **every aspect of our lives.** In this knowing and acceptance of your authentic self you **will not believe or accept anyone else** ' **dogma or dreams that's not your own.** Rose personally does not **accept anything** without doing her research; **analyzing everything first, then meditating on the facts then precede accordingly.** Her **TRUE GOD SPIRIT WITHIN** made her aware of an **ENORMOUS** amount of **PROFOUND EMPOWERING KNOWLEDGE /WISDOM** as of now she has about **4,000 books, plenty of audio and visual material on many topics. She was lead to books and authors she never was aware of.** Listing of some of these authors and book titles, see the **Divine Guidance section on page 151)**

In 1999, when she was in the bookstore buying four of Joseph Murphy's books,** she didn't feel inclined to purchase **Songs of God** an interpretation **of the Psalms in the Bible,** because of its title, and at the time she didn't like reading **the Bible** because most of the **mis-interpreted** it out of **ignorance** or **for self-serving purposes.** In most cases some people just don't know any better and **they unknowingly make scripture sound very negative, confusing, and very judgmental,** arousing feelings of fear, guilt, and unworthy especially about the females!** Nonetheless her inner Spirit /higher self), t told her to buy this book, her reply to (was she would purchase that one only if she could afford all four, when she arrived at the register to her surprise, she had enough money to purchase all four books. God will have her/his way if we don't resist. Ironically,   Songs of God was the one she started reading first. and she love this book and has gained enormous inner and over-standing of the true interpretation that really resonated with her True Spirit/Soul, Being align with her heart energy center, ENERGETIC INTENTION.

Rose is now researching, and studying the symbolism of the Bible more from a higher level of consciousness, not because some religious person, church, or traditional programming has instructed her to do so. She pays more attention to her dreams, life lessons and having more profound visions, trusting her innate vision (third-eye) really the first eye your natural intuition the Creator has blessed us all within ourselves, as embodiments of the CREATOR/GOD

"And you will seek me and find me, when you search for me with all your heart and I will be found by you declared the Lord. And I will restore your fortune and gather you from all nations and from all the places where I have driven you declared the Lord and I will bring you back to the place from where I sent you in exile."
-Jeremiah 29:13-14

If we stay open and allow Infinite Intelligence to work through us, there is something new to learn (remember) every day. Rose makes the effort to remain relaxed, poised, serene, and be teachable (Read Psalms 32:8). Knowing she is a child of the Creator and there is nothing or no one greater. After doing all she can about a situation, she surrendered everything to the Universe, not denying facts, new people information or resisting new experiences, and applying some basic common sense. REAL COMMON SENSE!

Everything that is alignment with the COSMIC FRQUENCY works out for the good of all.

1. When did you first begin to know your true SOUL Goddess /God within you? (We have both energies)

2. Have you always known there is a greater power, not man's religion or the things of this earth, guiding your life?

3. Are you still confused and searching outside of yourself?

"Now I urge you, brethren, keep your eyes on who causes dissension and hindrance contrary to the teaching which you learned and turned away from For such people are slaves, not of our lord [law], but of their own appetites, and by their smooth and flattering speech they deceive the hearts of the unsuspecting."   -Romans 16:17-18

When she give thanks for her blessings, she say, "Thank you Infinite Intelligence; we did it. The CREATOR works through us, we are LOVING, BEAUTIFUL, POWERFUL CO-CREATORS. We are moving through and releasing density energy of this third dimension. Rose feels many of us are in different phases/stages of ascension; everyone will not ascend at the same time as we know time. The old corrupt paradigm is coming to an end. It is now about regeneration and raising the consciousness to a higher dimension. She is continuously dying in consciousness to be renewed and reborn. She makes the effort to still in a loving frequency and live by applying universal laws in faith and trust one day at a time.

New Birth - The realization by man of his spiritual identity, with the fullness of power and glory that follows a birth is a coming into a state of being. Man first is born, or comes into a state of physical being; he thinks of himself as flesh, material. The "new birth" is the coming into a higher state of being that is alive to the fact that man is like God, one with God.   -Charles Fillmore (page 140)

"And then I will declare to them, I never knew you; depart from me, you who practice lawlessness." -Matt. 7:21-23

"O, I love thy law! It is my mediation all day."   -
Psalms 119:97

STUFFING is not necessary for our development. It is the result of violating spiritual Laws." -R. W.

On September 9, 2000, Rose surprised her guests at her 50th birthday (Earthday) party with a marriage ceremony, a marriage to her Higher-Self. She jumped the broom and her loving son Cliff, and her spiritual daughter Stacey performed the Kwanzaa candle lighting ceremony and recited the seven principles. It is a great and profound commitment to always love, honor and trust her Goddess Self, At that time she couldn't wait to turn fifty; now, she can't wait to become seventy to have another greater revelation celebration. It is always the seed that we sow (thoughts, beliefs, and feelings) that decides the nature of our product. The leader that you are searching for is within you. LOVE and Be TRUE to YOURSELF FIRST. Everything start with your thoughts!

This education system is not about you learning for empowerment (programming), it's only about you being TRAINED (mind control) to fit into their false Matrix to remain their slave only for money (paper), false Labels, Titles and you become addicted attach to material possession MATERIALISTIC ZOMBIES, look at the lines five hours or more before the store open to buy electronic gadgets and sneakers (rubber) etc. How can a person believe they are intelligent with all their degrees (just a piece of paper with writing on it) when they don't know Their True Powerful Goddess/God self.

"We have received not the Spirit of the world, but the Spirit of THE CREATOR some call God, that we know the things we need are freely given to us by God already."

Check the clip-BASHAR-The beginning of your HERO JOURNEY.

YOU ARE the Power! YOU ARE the MIRACLE! CREATE YOUR OWN DIVINE MATRIX.

WHEN YOU KNOW YOUR TRUESELF, YOU WILL KNOW GOD AND LOVE AND TRUST YOURSELF.

RE-AWAKENING INTO FREEDOM, CHRIST /COSMIC CONSCIOUSNESS

DON"T EVER GIVE UP ON YOUR DIVINE SELF!!!

NOTES

LEARNING TO REMEMBER!

DON"T WORRY BE JOYOUS!!!

PURSUIT YOUR DIVINE SELF!

Chapter 1

My Wake-up Call

WORDS TO THE WISE! This is a magnificent time, filled with amazing new opportunity. In life there are CHOICES and CONSEQUENCES. ALL YOUR TRUE ANSWERS ARE IN YOUR HEART, NOT THE MIND.

In March 1987, on a warm beautiful spring day with a cool breeze tingling the air, I decided to go see a dermatologist about removing a small callous on my right finger. My appointment at St. Barnabas Hospital was made a month prior because, once again, my beloved companion, Frank, insisted I have a doctor examine a very small lesion which was the size of a pimple near my left elbow. It had been there a few months, didn't appear to be getting any larger and only hurt when I bumped against something. It seemed insignificant to me; therefore I didn't let it preoccupy my thoughts. I was more concerned about my fingers looking good at that time I was vain. My fingernails always grew long and pretty and their maintenance was of the utmost importance then, I am) a self-taught fashion designer/seamstress. From cutting so much fabric, the friction from the scissors caused a callous on my finger. Yet, on this glorious sun-filled day with its warm rays bathing me in spirit and its cool breeze stirring gently and caressing my skin, nature seemed to validate how good I was feeling at that moment in time, Finally I was happy feeling some control of my life! Thankfully, my three children were never a source of my emotional and spiritual woes. They have been among my greatest blessings in life. They taught me many things about myself and the universe and what is true love. In spite of myself being a young, hurt, unloved and confused mother who made her share of mistakes. I am sorry for any pain I may have inflicted on them out of my ignorance, and pray they can forgive me. Now, I am growing spiritually on all levels, raising my frequency and

1

inner/over-standing and can be a better role model for them. Unfortunately, Growing up with my parents for me was **very damaging**, which I **attempt several suicide, attached an abusive marriage**, and other **unhealthy relationships**, after I ended the marriage. My victim state of consciousness/ frequency continued to attract more negative, toxic, and ignorant people, which resulted in a lot of fear based, destructive choices. Birds of the same feather flock together - an appropriate phrase for people who are vibrating on the same frequency. It has nothing to do with what people have or how they look, talk, or act on the outside; it's about what we are truly feeling internally and your true intend behind what you do. WE need to embrace, control and learn from our dark/shadow side, to truly heal from within for empowerment.

After coming through those challenges and being able to stand on the other side in glory, I finally began to feel my power and some control! Unbeknownst to me, I was about to face a prognosis that would change my entire life forever...not just for myself, but for all of humanity...and provide me with a golden opportunity to learn and actually remember God's truth. Not by listening to so-called preachers with their screaming (like James Brown's song says, "Talking loud and saying nothing") jumping and dancing. I had this golden opportunity, if I was willing to accept change and take a stand for God's truth, to learn, grow, love, live, free my mind, and risk not being a slave any longer. Freedom of mind is worth dying for because without it, you are really in a hypnotic state which is susceptible to mind control (a robot). I needed and found the courage to stand, even when it meant standing alone and not conforming to anyone else's beliefs or guidelines for acceptance. No! I didn't know at that time I could stand up to the challenge! Later, I achieved a knowing that no man could stop what is divinely yours in divine order and time, if you apply universe laws and trust. I went to my appointment at St. Barnabas Hospital that beautiful day in March (the date indelibly etched in my mind) that would profoundly change my life forever. I sat in the waiting room, pondering about the callous on my finger and wondered what course of action the doctor would take all the while still not concerned with the small lesion on my elbow. My initial reaction when seeing the callous was, "Oh, no! This is spoiling my beautiful hands," I assumed once the doctor assessed my callous he would schedule me an appointment to have it removed and that would be it. It was warm in the waiting room, which prompted me to remove the light jacket I was wearing. In hindsight, I now know that subtle and seemingly inconsequential action was initiated by Divine HIGHER CONSCIOUSNESS.

After an hour wait, this slim, tall, attractive, and nice Indian doctor beckoned me into his office, what a relief! I was beginning to become anxious simply wanting the examination to be over. While showing him the callous and inquiring as to how soon he would be able to remove it, I noticed he was paying more attention to my arm than my finger. He seemed to be obsessed with the small sore on my left elbow. With the incomparable sizes of the two the lesion being as small as a pimple and the callous being twenty times that size, I was baffled with his interest, especially when he said, "I'm more concerned with the sore on your elbow." He then asked me, "How long has it been there?" Instantly, I replied, "About three months." He then inquired, "Are there any more lesions like this on your body?" "No," was my answer, which prompted him to ask, "Have you been coughing with any shortness of breath or chest pain?" I thought for a second, and then realizing that I have had chest pain, I exclaimed "Yes! There has been some coughing and shortness of breath too."

My mind wrapped around the possibility that something had triggered the re-occurrence of the asthma during my child-hood. However, the realization for my beloved Frank's urgent concern about the one lesion

3

was about to come true. The doctor then inquired if he could take a biopsy of the sore, and stated that he believed I had a disease that was incurable but treatable. He named three possible diseases and the sound of his voice magnified the alarm of distress going off in my head. All I wanted him to do was to shut up! The possibility of something seriously assaulting my body, fear set in and a sinking feeling in my stomach. When the doctor didn't list AIDS among the possibilities, I was somewhat relieved. AIDS was in the forefront of the human psyche during that time, fueling fear of the inevitable suffering and death. I remember thinking it couldn't be **AIDS**, I hadn't had that many sex partners. I was reminded of the mantra, "It only takes one." In a moment of frivolity probably, I felt cheated and thought, if I am going to die, at least I should have had more sexual liaisons. (Just joking)! I reflected on the fact the diseases the doctor had mentioned were not familiar to me: Sarcoma, Lupus, and Sarcoidosis. At the time of my revelation I was fearful of the unknown, as most of us are. He performed the biopsy afterward to return in two weeks for the results, walking home I ruminated on the possibilities of the results, could this all be true? And if it was, what was I going to do about it? How would it affect my life, my children, parents, mate, and close friends? I started envisioning the worst scenarios with the ultimate ending in death. This negative outlook was predictable for an individual who grew up in bleak circumstances and I possessed the mindset that resulted from such chaos. The people in my intimate circle reflected back to me the worst possible scenarios with their superimposed imprints of fear, denial, ignorance, superstition, negative thought and speech patterns, doom belief credos and religious dogma, all infused with fears, quilt, mass conformity of this false construct and victim consciousness. Thinking on this low vibration frequency scared me more than the possible disease my body was hosting. Feeling scared

4

I decided not to tell anyone **what the doctor suspected**, only **Frank** was aware of my appointment with the doctor, and **I decided to lie to him.**

Coupled with this new determination to conceal it was a **strong sense of denial,** this diagnosis couldn't be true when everything in my life was on an upswing. **The mere thought was overwhelming,** and my **anxiety** was heightened because I wasn't sure if I had the **strength or courage to face and conquer this attack/growth lesson..** When I reassessed all I had gone through earlier in my life, all the **adversity** that had **previously crossed my path, I was reminded of my resilience** to resolve obstacles and a personal growth occurred with each challenge conquered and most importantly, I was still standing. Consequently, I decided to continue my life as if nothing were encroaching upon it. Not **facing the fear** is the **social normal** (ESCAPISM), in two weeks I returned to the hospital alone, **still praying and hoping the biopsy was just a fluke.** As I entered the doctor's office, the look on his face told me the results were **positive.** Of the three aforementioned diseases, **the doctor confirmed it was Sarcoidosis,** and it **was infiltrating my skin.** He wanted to conduct a **variety of tests to determine if other organs** have been affected. He **was certain my lungs had been assaulted, too. He** explained there was no known cause for this disease. It could only be treated wherever it nested, and it couldn't be halted from affecting additional organs. Accompanied by sadness in his voice, he showed compassion, but it wasn't what I wanted to hear or was willing to accept, especially the word "incurable." EVERY THING IS ENERGY

Fear and emotional damage imprisoned me once again, and I wanted to scream! Instead I cried, which resulted in me feeling a little better. I departed from his office, my future was being filled with appointments for numerous tests, eye examinations, pulmonary inspections, chest x-rays, blood extractions, and heart cardiograms, which were just the tip of the iceberg. Feeling afraid, alone, and desperate after leaving the hospital that day, I bellowed out to God, "WHY ME?" The mere cry for TRUE GOD raises one's consciousness, and not man or his religious dogma. Unfortunately, I didn't know by embracing the fear/shadow side and learning what I needed from it, indicated my soul was ready to receive from the **COSMIC GUIDELINE.** That day I heard my **true Spirit of God within** for the first time with enormous clarity, deep in my soul; I heard the **still whisper of a voice inside** that rattled me to the **core** of my being, the voice said, "**Why not you?** You **asked** for a disease, baffled I thought, what kind of an answer is that from the **PRIME CREATOR,** known by many names.

Why would anyone ask for a disease? Then, I thought God might be punishing me for some so-called sin I didn't remember committing. Raised in a traditional false religious setting, I believed God may have pity on me because of my earnest attempts to do the right things. According to the **religious people** around me at the time, **I considered myself a good person who always made an effort to help others.** Therefore it was **incomprehensible why I was experiencing this disease, pain, and other forms of suffering. The religious** stalwarts said it was **God's will or the Devil's** which was also **incomprehensible** since **PRIME CREATOR/GOD** loves all her/his children unconditionally and gave us free will and wants only the best for all of us. I was still trapped in the mind program. I also read in the Bible: "I am come that they might have life and they might have it more abundantly." -John 10:10

I completed the medical tests; two weeks later received the results. It was confirmed that my lungs were also affected, the other tests were negative. The doctor stated I had a healthy and strong heart, and he was very efficient in explaining the treatment plan he wanted to implement, which included monthly visits on an outpatient basis. Also with the **frequent monitoring of my health status,** it would be necessary to receive steroid shots in each lesion, and I would have to take a prednisone pill every day for the rest of my life. I was still afraid of the possible effects this condition could wreak on my body and was dismayed by the shadow of uncertainty which was clouding my future. Although all of the above was looming overhead, I was still grateful no other organs had been impaired. **Pain and dis-eases are the body's way of letting us know something EMOTIONALLY, MENTALLY, PHYSICALLY, and SPIRITUALLY is wrong (OUT OF BALANCE) inside of us. Marching or Walking is not the cure!**

Sarcoidosis may have no symptoms depending on what tissues or organs of the body that are affected. If the lungs are affected, you may have shortness of breath and the scar tissue from the disease may lead to bacterial infections or bronchitis. Other organs and tissues which may be affected are the liver, lymph glands, spleen, skin, eyes, and bones in the hands and feet. It is an inflammatory dis-ease. (Do your own research)

Check out the clip on youtube-
BLOOD REPROGRAMMING.
Shaki Gawain: Creative Visualization

A must see DVD: THE LIVING MATRIX, a film on the new science of (SPIRITUAL HEALING).

Chapter 2
Denial

After receiving the results of the medical tests, I left St. Barnabas Hospital got on a bus headed straight to Montefiore or Jacobi hospital's emergency for a second opinion. When asked the reason for my visit I pretended not to know what was wrong with me. I explained to the nurse I was experiencing some chest pains and just wanted a chest x-ray, as you can guess them too, wanted to perform a series of tests, I insisted on only a chest x-ray. The doctor looked at me suspiciously, as if he knew I knew what the test would convey. At this point a confirmation of the first test's results was necessary; I didn't care what they were thinking.

Although the number of people seeking medical assistance in the emergency room was enormous, treatment moved swiftly; waiting for the x-ray results didn't take long, sitting on the examination room table awaiting a new fate, I anchored myself in prayer, hoping, but doubting at the same time, my lungs were clear and that I didn't have Sarcoidosis or anything else. That mode of conflict (praying and doubting) is normal when one is raised around people who say they have faith, but unconsciously do not truly believe or know what faith is, most people deny their true feelings and the reality of their life model that was shown to us. Therefore, denying I was ill was easier than accepting that something was wrong. After all, if I denied the Sarcoidosis or any other problems, then I didn't have to do anything about it, and if I accepted it as a real affliction that I wanted and was ready to rid myself of, now I HAVE TO do something To RAISE MY FREQUENCY. The people of my world were living a lie, pretending everything was fine and they were happy. Out of false fears and religious beliefs, limitations, ignorance, feeling powerless, and waiting on someone called Jesus or whoever to save them from themselves which was not for me! I now wanted and needed true answers that made sense for me, because every effect has a cause and we need to take responsibility for what we have created consciously or unconsciously. EVERYTHING IS VIBRATING.

Most of us chose to believe the lies. Denial is a very strong psychological mechanism that keeps and aiding us in making excuses for not really doing something significant about our situation. When we resist change, we pay a high price. When we are denying, justifying, or projecting on others and making excuses that something is not psychologically wrong in our self and our lives, we are compounding the situation. In this state of denial, we attempt to alleviate painful symptoms with inappropriate medical treatments, with the use of medications that don't address the core cause of the disease, they only treat the symptoms. By running to organized religious institutions, we just add to the massive numbers of disillusioned individuals who gather in fear, guilt, doubt, low self-esteem, inferiority, insecurity, and powerlessness trying to sugarcoat their conditions in life, denying the truth about what we really feel about ourselves. You can't truly heal or resolve problems on the physical   level, when the causes are on the mental   and   Spiritual   level   a   divine   imbalance. WE must live by NATURE/COSMIC GUIDELINES

I am working continually on my all levels of my INNER DIVINE SELF every day now, changing and letting go of all illusions and anything or anyone that imprison my soul. DON'T BELIEVE THE HYPE!

MATERAILISM WANTS are used to keep us in CONFORMITY for MIND CONTROL.

9

Chapter 3
The Power of Words

"I say to you that every careless word that men shall speak, they shall render account for it in the Day of Judgment; for by your words you shall be justified, and by your words you shall be condemned."
-Matthew 12:36-37

We are raised in a world of deception and subliminal negative messages that give us a limited false perception of our true selves and what is really happening all around us. This creates false feelings of powerlessness, low self-esteem, unworthiness, fear, and guilt. Majority of these negative messages reach the masses by ways of negative television programming, radio talk shows, movies, mis-education, books, magazines, computer games, institutionalized false religious and spiritual groups, politics, and negative advertising. All of these are used to manipulate the listeners; thus, dis-empowering people from raising their consciousness and frequency from the lowest pit of hell. We buy things we don't really need, want, or cannot afford at the time, while trying to hide our inferiority and desperately trying to fill a false emptiness inside with non-benevolent substances the system imposes in our psyche. As a result, we give up our true power and accept their propaganda such as the AMERICAN DREAM, NOT THE CREATOR (GOD) PROMISE.

Here is a list of some of the negative phrases used and their true underlining meanings to me.

"He who walks with the wise men will be wise, but the companion of fools will suffer harm." -Proverbs 13:20

"It's too good to be true" - Implying that we don't really deserve something that good. Having Divine good is your birth right.

"You have to see it to believe it" - No! You have to believe it and you'll see it. If we decree something great, in divine order we will get it. Trust is what true prayer is. (Pro.23:7)

"There is not enough" - There is no lack in the universe.

"Your body falls apart after age 40" - Not true, if you take proper care of your body, the body will take care of you

"Opportunity knocks only once" - Creates limitations that you don't get a second chance. The universe is abundant with opportunities. We need to program our mind to see the opportunities that are continually presenting themselves.

"It's too late" – Creates a false sense of helplessness. "Where there's a will, there's a way." We have all the qualities we attribute to GOD -love, power, wisdom, compassion, peace wealth, etc. it's not too late for God to do something, God works through us.

"Don't get too happy; it won't last" - Creates fear of true happiness, lack and discomfort. We continually give attention and power to whatever negative beliefs are in our unconscious mind; thus, allowing what we don't want to manifest in our life. It is our birthright to re-claim our true DIVINE JOY!

"Without a so call good education, you cannot succeed" NOT TRUE. Many have succeeded without that SLAVE VALIDATION piece of paper. Like Dave Thomas, CEO of Wendy's, and Malcolm X, who truly educated himself in prison and many more successful people.

"You're too old" - Creates false limitation. I'm sure you've heard of people in their 60's, even 90's who went back to school, got married, or started a new career or business and overcame challenging obstacle..

11

"Life is a struggle" - Affirms that life has to be hard. We should think of life as a **learning experience for Soul awakening and an adventure** not a struggle.

"You're stupid" - They are **implying** that we cannot learn. However, you can if you were not **mis-educated** by design to keep you a working slave in some form for this **system SLAVE PLANTATION for life.**

"Something is wrong with you, if you don't conform" - To the contrary, you need to learn how to be your unique true self in order to **be really fulfilled and happy inside and out.**

"Keep the dream alive" – What about making your dreams, SOUL MISSION and VISIONS your REALITY.

"Don't ask questions" - Just accept that whatever you are told is true? No! Question everything. Do deep research. Discover things for yourself and arrive at your own truth.

"The struggle continues" - We repeatedly **reverberate** those words in our minds. **That's why the struggle doesn't stop! Words are** powerful; use them wisely.

"Everyone has problems" - So you must have them, too? **We have** challenges, lessons, and Opportunities and consequences to learn and grow, not problems.

"Everyone gets sick" - This implies that sickness is normal. No, it's abnormal! Just because something is going around why do you have to catch it?!

"It's God's Will" - Creates the **illusion** that we have **no** responsibility for **our choices in life only when it good.**

"Original Sin" – (aka "You're born in sin") a negative, misinterpreted and false teaching that creates feelings of unworthiness and guilt. Read; The Original Blessing- by Matthew Fox.

"Someone died for your sins" - Creates feelings of guilt, obligation, shame, and fear.

"You've got the Devil in you" - Not true. We are created in the image and likeness of the Creator. God is the only true HIGHER power. Everything else is an illusion; evil darkness is real because we gave it power. GOD is energy dark and light! We choose whom we will serve.

"God is a jealous God" –She/he has no reason to be jealous because everything is GOD's, and she/he would not have given us free will to choose.

"God will punish you" - What happened to unconditional love and free will? We punish ourselves by our thoughts, feelings and actions.

"God is an angry God" - Isaiah 27:4 refutes this: "Fury is not in me."

"You need to fear God" - The word "fear" had a different meaning in Biblical days. What the phrase really means is you need to have revere for God.

"Money is evil" - Then why do all the preachers, bishops popes, churches, religious and spiritual institutions want it more than anything? It's really about how we use it.

"Illness runs in your family" - This negative programming in the unconscious mind, that is pasted down for generations.

"The word 'incurable'" - Anything is possible   (Read Mark 17:20). "Vote or Die" - Black people during the 1960's were being killed while trying to vote. Voting creates the false illusion that man (politicians), not

13

The true Spirit within, which is the source we MUST TOTALLY depend on for everything. Voting is a distraction from the CREATOR. If you are going to vote, WE NEED TO VOTE IN THE CONSCIOUSNESS OF PRIME CREATOR/GOD.

"Fashion label "State Property" - Implies that you belong to the state. This imprisons the mind, which is worse than imprisonment of the body.

Negative messages are designed to degrade the person and perpetuate unworthiness, low self-esteem, stupidity, inferiority, etc. Adding to the fray are people who wear t-shirts with negative slogans that state: "Treat Me Like a Slut," "100% Bitch," "I Am No Angel," "If You Think I'm A Bitch, You Should Meet My Mother," "If You're Rich, I'm Your Bitch," (Now, what real man would want someone who thinks so low of herself?), and this one "Get Rich or Die Trying". What is the latter really saying to someone who lives with low income or none and lives in poverty? It's really sad that most black people have let this system convince them that they are worthless; thus, allowing themselves to be over consumers and adorned in such negative slogans. Unfortunately, not only are they adorning themselves in these negative phrases, most people, all form of entertainers are also creating them and voluntarily aiding in the perpetuation of this genocidal onslaught Read: Born brain dead (lost books of Africa rediscovered by Dr. Khalid Al Mansour.

"Believe nothing, no matter where you read it or who said it. No matter if I have said it, unless it agrees with your own reason and your "common sense."   -Buddha

Instead of combining our energies into seemingly positive symbols like wearing ribbons against cancer, walking, marching, or making strides against any disease, let's utilize that same energy to focus on health prevention, abundant wealth and wholeness. We will then see larger

14

cases of healthy people because there is greater power in unified numbers. Energy is more powerful than money. (A must see DVD: The Death of Black America by-Dr. Llaila Africa and Death by Medicine by- Gary Null and many more, do your research. Movie: SICKO - by M. Moore

We volunteer with good intentions, but wrong method. We promote causes when we really don't over-stand exactly what the **subliminal** message is or what the true intent is behind these causes. (Reverse psychology) Due to the ignorance of our consciousness we manifests things, we contribute to the unhealthiness of people by expending our energies and contributing financial support. The real challenge is to raise our level of consciousness and **balance right brain,** a region in the brain where **health solutions** can be manifest **to help change something** that is wrong, injustice, to make a **profound change in the lives and** others. Self-reflect, meditate on this every day for at least nine or twenty-one days, and see what revelations are revealed about you.

Back in the day "positive thought provoking" manifested itself in our music with singers like Marvin Gaye singing "What's Going On," Teddy Pendergrass' "Wake Up Everybody," Curtis Mayfield's "Dirty Laundry in the Country," The O'Jays' "For the Love Of Money," and Bob Marley's "Get Up Stand Up." Lauryn Hill for her song- "The Lost Ones" Sly and the family stone- "STAND." They sang about what was wrong in this system. Interestingly now these things still prevalent today, even WORSE with so much more NEGATIVE ENTERTAINMENT.

THE CONTROLLING DECEIVERS numbs your mind and close your heart by simulating only your five senses by insulting your true Intelligent/wisdom with non-sense that is mostly all kind of INTERTAINMENT, FALSE HOLIDAYS, OVERING EATING,

DRINKING, SHOPPING, SEX and COMPETITION. (You know the list)

What are you willing to give up, to live FREE and reclaim your DIVINE POWER?

Make a list, Go into the silence within you, and meditate and listen to that still soft voice in your HEART/SOUL.

Below, describe negative messages that you are aware of and how they adversely affect your life. What lies do you tell yourself everyday? Be honest with yourself.

When negative subliminal messages, images are impressed and stored in the subconscious mind, they will manifest sooner or later, no matter how good we may think we are at suppressing them. It doesn't matter what label, if we are a so-called Spiritual, Christian, Buddhist, Muslim, Jehovah's Witness, Seventh Day Adventist, Baptist, Catholic, or any other religion. The fact remains that man's has been hypnotized. If you do not control your subconscious mind, someone else will. God created humans by the power of her/his word and man is a co-Creator using that same energy power constructively or destructively. Unplug from the false matrix- **ILLUSION OF INCLUSION**. Every thought and word we speak continuously with strong feelings causes a vibration in the Universe's Energy Field. The effects of that vibration will return in direct accordance with the nature of the word. In the beginning was the sound (frequency).

"After He called the multitude to Him, He said to them hear and understand, 'Not what enters into the mouth defiles the man, but what proceeds out of the mouth, this defiles the man."   -Proverbs 18:21

I don't sing or listen to gospel music "Specially Amazing Grace" anymore once I looked up the meaning of the word "WRETCH." The Webster's dictionary meaning of the word is: despicable; profoundly unhappy; a miserable and vile person. This description does not fit what God has created. Everything that God created in its true essence is good. **Slave owner John Newton wrote the song, he was talking about himself.**   (Do your research).

"You are children of the most highest." John 10:34

BEING WEALTHY AND FREE IS YOUR BIRTHRIGHT!

17

Chapter 4
Facing the Fear

When the two **Montefiore Hospital emergency room** doctors returned, they didn't have to say a word. The look on their faces told me what I didn't want to hear again. They looked at me with **compassion and said, "You already know."** I mustered up a **little smile trying to hold back the tears, while nodding my head yes.** The better part of my earlier life was spent **crying; feeling depressed, and feels like a victim. Sadness, loneliness, disappointment, hurt and being engulfed in emotional and mental pain. My cup had runneth** over with more **pain and sorrow for long enough.** When was my life ever going to resemble the **"bliss of normalcy"** that other people **effortlessly seem to take for** granted. **Don't just existing, start living YOUR life now!**

The diagnosis and treatment the doctors mapped out for me was the same. This is where my "bliss of normalcy" resides. **Fortunately, their bedside manner was earnestly pleasant. I informed them I was going back to St. Barnabas to start the treatment there because they had already completed all of the necessary tests.** The Montefiore doctors extended the option to me to return if, for any reason, I wasn't happy with the care at St. Barnabas. I left there feeling I could handle this situation; something was stirring within me, **awakening me to a higher consciousness, a surge of courage, strength, and believe it or not a sense of peace consumed me, what was happening at this time in my life was exactly what was needed scarier as it was.** I just had to **now inner and over-stand the lessons I needed to learn from this experience,** and **what Prime creator was revealing to me. MY PURSUIT OF TRUESELF!**

Chapter 5
Not Recognizing the Answer

I began treatment, taking steroid shots every month and a daily pill of Motrin 800mg for the pain. When, I arrived home from my first monthly outpatient clinic treatment. I RECEIVED A TRUE DIVINE MESSENGER FROM PRIME CREATOR.

On April of 1987, I was greeted by a TRUE servant of the TRUTH. Another nice warm sun-filled spring day, the block was bustling with human's energy, smiles were abundant, and experiencing the glory of the day was my main objective. I was greeted with warm smiles and sweet hello from individuals who had no idea of the challenge I was presently facing. Upon reaching my apartment building, a familiar voice called out my name, it was my neighbor **Benji**, from Trinidad, a petite man of dark complexion, mixed gray hair, and whose face was always lit by his radiant smile, and he loved to consume alcohol, had several missing teeth, he possessed only a third-grade education. Being a handyman his clothing was often covered with splattered paint stains. However, all of that is inconsequential to his heart of gold and the wisdom he bestows on everyone he meets. He was a real thinker and has a true God loving Spirit.

Wisdom - Intuitive knowing, spiritual intuition; the voice of God within as the source of our understanding; mental action based on the Christ truth within. Wisdom includes judgment, discrimination, intuition, and all the departments of mind that come under the head of knowledge.

"Spiritual discernment always places wisdom above the other faculties of the mind and reveals that knowledge and intelligence are auxiliary to understanding."   -Charles Fillmore (page 211)

Upon hearing Benji call out to me, I didn't want to talk to anyone, I felt like a fish out of water in an unfamiliar situation feeling empty inside. I turned and nonchalantly said, "What do you want?" There he stood in a good disposition, smiling, laughing, and unruffled by my rudeness. "I got this little book for you," He revealed to me that a dear friend of his named Karim, who was a Muslim and lived in our building at the time, gave him this book Benji told me he said to himself, who can I give this book to that would benefit and do the most good with it?" And his answer was me. The book entitled The Key to Yourself by -Venice Bloodworth was one of the original copies, which had seen over thirty years of wear and tear, with yellowish-brown pages separating from its spine. That one act of someone giving me something altered my mood greatly. After thanking Benji I scurried to my apartment. Unwinding and relishing my solitude, I re-examined the book just given to me and thought; I need a book right now like I need a hole in the head. I wanted immediate answers to my problem, anxious and dissatisfied, God was informed by me that I was not living or dying with this disease. I started fumbling through some of its pages, and then put it down, picked it open again not focusing, then deciding it was of no real value to me, so I thought!

"He shall call upon me, and I will answer him: I will be with him in trouble; I will deliver him, and honor him with long life. With long life will I satisfy him, and show him my salvation" -Psalms 91:15-16

I started my treatment while still not fully understanding my condition. Now that all the attention was on the disease the little sore rapidly multiplied and grew, while the pain in my lungs and skin worsen, each visit to the clinic brought back to me the startling reality of my condition. I was confronted head on with people who had the same dis-ease but were in various stages. Although I tried not to focus too much on the other patients, I couldn't help but notice people walking with oxygen tanks, inhalers, and wandering in the corridors with visible sores on their bodies and faces. It would be less than a year before the lesions spread over my face, the cheeks, ears, extending to my right eyebrow, the tip of my nose, and over various areas of my body mainly the joint areas. After a couple of weeks passed I decided to tell Frank, my children, and other family members what was going on with me. Seeing the hurt, sadness, and helplessness in their eyes, I was shattered emotionally. In a brief time span, their fear morphed into sympathy and uncertainty instead of empathy. Although everyone wanted to help, they didn't know how. This is why telling them was so DIFFICULT.

I called my best friend, Dorothy to tell her about my prognosis. She was still working at a book company I once worked for too. She was very loving, supportive and helpful. She sent me a copy of The American Medical Association Family Health Guide which included some information about **Sarcoidosis** and basically collaborated with the information I previously heard. The health guide stated that in some cases, the dis-ease goes into remission, and this gave me some hope later I started receiving negative information, hearing about a few individuals that died from the dis-ease and how it spread to the brain, the liver, the bones, and eyes, which caused loss of eyesight. You can imagine how my emotional state fluctuated as I tried to understand the prognosis. My mother's reaction to my situation was in accordance with her conditioning and programming, she asked me to go to her church to obtain counseling from her pastor and allow him to pray for me. As I sat there with my mother and her pastor at the Soul Saving Station Church, all I could feel and hear was something stirring deep from within, saying, "I sent you the answer, trust! read the book **Benji** gave you internalize every word, meditate over and over until you over- stand its wisdom, and then apply that true empowering wisdom to your life that gives results. Restoring TRUE LOVE FAITH and TRUST! Mark- 5:34, your faith has healed you.

I put the book aside at this time, I found myself where I said I didn't want to be hoping with wishing but hoping my mother's pastor could pray or do something to get God to heal me. Hmm, if her pastor or anyone that's supposed to know God could heal me, then there would be no need for me to learn why and how I created this dis-ease and take responsibility to do the internal work and heal myself. Leaving their so-called House of God, I intuitively knew my desire to be healed was not going to be realized as long as I continued to see myself as a victim and looked to someone else to heal or save me really from myself. I now know the House of God is not found in a man-made building, our bodies are the living temple. Why do we believe God talks and listen to these famous so called spiritual leaders, preachers and not us. In God's eye all divine spirits are equal, powerful and her/his children are a divine SOUL in a vessel.

I was very grateful for my mother's desire to help me the only way she knew and for her pastor's time, I had no inherent desire to find solace in the church, and couldn't pretend to, that was largely due to the suffering of patrons of the church, especially as a young girl, the prolonged illnesses suffered by my maternal grandmother and others. They were constantly praying to a Jesus that never seemed to answer their wails or woe which made me think as a child God couldn't hear or there was something wrong with the concept. There were too many contradictions with most religion teaching. I now realize that they were not praying in the truest sense of faith, because prayer is affirming and knowing without a doubt you will get what you decree with strong feeling and what is in divine order and time, for example, "I feel and I am healthy," and "I am healed," not supplications such as, "God, I am sick. Please heal me." I believe they had faith in their religion, but not in the creator because they really didn't know or understand what and who this infinite energy force known by many difference names some call God. Luke 18:42 "THY FAITH HAS HEALED THEE"

"Thou shall have no other gods before me." Which simply means, don't worship any person, place, or thing, only the Christ within you.

In summary, I realized I had to give all of my allegiance to the one creative power that resides within. If you think someone other than you or some building has a greater influence with the creator than you, you are WORSHIPING an IDOL; you are as CLOSE to GOD as your thinking, beliefs, feelings or attitudes permit.

I was now experiencing a true death and resurrection on this physical level. The True Re-Birthing

The Courage to be Free!

MY TRUE SPRIRT /HEART and SOUL don't want to ever be confined/ trap or imprison to any person, place or any piece of paper, a title, book or building. Free your mind and your body and spirit will follow, and you will always be in harmony with your true Spirit. I contemplate Infinite Intelligence every day, not just on Friday, Saturday, Sunday, or so-called religious holidays that are commercialized for more greed, energy and mind control. WAKE-UP!

Read: Freedom from the Known by-Krishnam

DID YOU PASS YOUR DIVINE TESTS!!!

My Nine Necessary Conditions for TRUE PRAYER Focus, Meditation, Contemplation, Communion & Communication)

1. Get very still, relax, and go into deep breathing then in complete silence of your subconscious mind.

2. The Creator should be recognized as an energy force referred to as Heavenly Father and Holy Mother or Mother Earth.

3. Oneness with the Creator should always be affirmed.

4. Prayer must be made within your heart...the subconscious mind referred to as the secret place.

5. The conscious mind must be focused on what you want, not what you don't want.

6. Affirm what you need, deserve and visualize it.

7. When you pray, you must believe you have received it.

8. The Kingdom of the Creator must be your number one priority, not money and material things.

9. Always be thankful in the present and affirm out loud with strong emotions, Listen to the clip on youtube- with MANLY P. HALL – VICTORY OF THE SOUL OVER CIRCUMSTANCE.

PRIME CREATOR" will is done.

TRUST! SURRENDER and LET GO! MOST PEOPLE ARE UNCONSCIOUS ADDICTED TO NEGATIVITY, PAIN, DRAMA AND ALL KIND OF SUFFERING.

Words of Growth

To dare to laugh is to risk appearing the fool.

To weep is to risk appearing sentimental.

To reach for another is to risk involvement.

To expose your ideas and your dreams before a crowd is to risk their loss.

To love is to risk not being loved in return.

To truly live is to risk to unplugging and dying.

To believe is to risk failure. But risks must be taken, because the greatest hazard in life is to risk nothing.

The people who risk nothing of real value feel like nothing deep inside. They may avoid some suffering and sorrow, but they cannot truly learn, feel, change, grow, or truly love, and live their full potential life PURPOSE. Chained by their attitudes, false fears and ego they are still SLAVES; they have forfeited their FREEDOM.

Only a person who takes DIVINE RISKS for their SOUL PURPOSE is TRULY FREE.   -
(Unknown author, altered by Rose Whaley)

Check out by-BASHAR-Breaking free from EGO.

LOVE! PEACE AND JOY. NOT FEAR, HATE, MISEY, WAR AND SUFFERING.

Later in May, on a Sunday evening, I felt dis-enchanted with conventional solutions and felt pushed to read the book Benji had given me. Opening it and skimming its pages, I felt compelled to make sense of its words. As I read from page to page internalizing every word my awareness grew; awakening my subconscious mind and a new feeling of self-empowerment started too welled up within me with each successive word understood, I felt more deeply at peace. I couldn't believe such a little book would provide such empowering information and would ignite that which I thought was lost to myself, which had yet to be authentically defined.

My soul was finally being fed by ideas that were unknown (forgotten) to me, due to my conformity with mass consciousness. I was being taught a mystical idea that everything I ever needed or will ever need already resides within me. This idea was revolutionary, something not introduced at schools that were responsible for teaching us how to think instead of what to think, institutions of religion that were supposed to teach how to know GOD, truth within ourselves, In their bible it says "GOD said I have written in the hearts of man". TI DIDN'T SAY IN A BOOK. And this system, religion, family culture, and community members that tried to mold my Spirit and its Infinite Wisdom to their beliefs. I had always been taught to look outside myself for answers. I was reminded by one of the true masters teaches. He taught, "Everything you need is right within you." So simple that it escapes most of us even though it is repeated: "Look, don't look here, don't look there The Kingdom of Heaven is within you." What I really needed was not in a mate, Pastor, Bishop, the Pope, the Clergy, the First Lady, the Prime Minister, the President, or Celebrity or material things; and it definitely were not in symbols such as: academic degrees, crosses, robes, special buildings, or statues. All these things have meaning of very little substance and no real value in the spiritual realm. We must remember that all are beckoned to inner and over-stand that we are everything. Very few actually achieve this higher frequency of knowing Christ /God Consciousness. I believe that Infinite Intelligence answers all prayers. We don't recognize the answers due to our false programming; we expect them to come in a specific way and from a specific person related to some religion. Therefore, out of fear and not wanting to admit that what we believe may be wrong, we resist, deny, fight against, and run from the truth when it comes to us in an unexpected or unfamiliar way. As a result, we end up missing the true answer that would free our minds and hearts forever.

I thought I have learned a lot in my thirty-five years of existing, (not living). The book; Key to Yourself awakened me up to a new level of knowing and over-standing of empowering knowledge, which is ancient wisdom. It taught me how to think (remember), something which is not very common in today's world.

"If you give a man a fish, he won't go hungry today, but if you teach a man to fish, he'll eat forever." (Really teach people who they truly are WITHIN, DIVINE and POWERFUL.

Schools taught me basic academics; religious institutions illustratively sketched the people, places, and events from their limited and false interpretation of the Bible; yet, no one taught me who I truly am in reference to my true Spirit and Soul. I had never been told that God and I are one - the God within, that embodied everything and everywhere. We as a collective consciousness must stop allowing others to implant a false Spirits in us. The Soul in you is true cause, completely sovereign, and should be the only ruler over our lives; not any religion, church, group, person, condition, pain, or external thing such as fear, guilt, anxiety, worry, limitation, ignorance, a comfort zone, titles, or labels, status quo and materialism and the list goes on. Some of the chapter titles in this easy read book are: "The Law of Attraction, Superconscious mind, Subconscious Mind, The Universal (God) Mind, True Faith," "Sowing the Seed," "Disease," "The Importance of the Silence," "It is Never Too Late," "True Prosperity," and "The Word of Power." This wisdom rang true in my consciousness, but the most significant lesson I learned from this little book was the strength and beauty of self-love, Universal Love, and just being true to myself which in the beginning was a huge challenge. I continued reading and being amazed by my ability to comprehend the ideas being put forth, it felt as if they had always been with me and I just needed to be awakened from my slumber to embrace them again, everything became clearer in this realm of inner and over- standing. Infinite Intelligence always assigns someone, somewhere, to truly help us to reconnect to the truth.

If we are really ready to change old negative, limited patterns and come out of our conformist patterns of thinking and being, we can then solve what we think is a problem. It's about growing spiritually and remembering who we truly are. It's about growing spiritually and remembering all divine spirit is a manifestation of the CREATOR/GOD in the flesh. If and when people are really ready and willing to change, an ill person can get a good doctor or spiritual healer or both. A drowning person gets a rope or lifejacket. A person with a computer problem seeks out a technician. A true student gets a true teacher. A person with a spiritual problem, which is the cause of all so-called problems, gets a true prophet. A true prophet is one who receives inspiration from true Spirit, who inner/over-stands spiritual laws and imparts it to others to awaken and empower them. The Bible says, "Beware of false prophets," (Matthew 7:15) deceptive thoughts built up by errors and selfish desires.

"False prophets are the representatives of deceptive religious thoughts. They appear to be innocent and harmless like sheep, but in reality are selfish and dangerous. They come in pretty packages, dressed in rich beautiful robes or suits and may use fancy big words, but inwardly, they are ravenous, like wolves." -Charles Fillmore (page 157)

I got the spiritual teacher, the way to heal, the lifejacket, and a true prophet all at once, that's why Benji was assigned to me by the Creator of all things to give me that old raggedy little book. I thank Infinite Intelligence every day for that blessed occurrence. Now I over-stand Psalms 37:11, "But the meek shall inherit the earth and shall delight themselves in the abundance of peace." Biblically speaking, the word "meek" represents a mind that is teachable, open, receptive, and possessing a faith in God (Universal Mind), with the awareness that the Will of the Infinite for you is always something magnificent, glorious, joyous, and vital. What comes to mind is the old oriental saying, "Meek compels God herself, not man."

We all feel that we are seeking true spiritual fulfillment. We don't know the difference between true spirituality and false religion or anything else. False Religion is a desensitizing substitute. It's the absence of the Infinite Intelligence, True Spirit! We abandoned our spiritual values and worship celebrities and preachers to define our self-worth (that why they are highly PAID to sell us lies, and don' paid taxes), this material and physical world which created a damaging narcissistic culture. How many painful roads must we travel down before admitting we are truly lost SOULS? (DIS-CONNECTED FROM SOURCE / TRUESELF)

29

One day during my monthly clinic appointment, two other doctors asked me if they could look at the lesions on my face and body. They said the sores were unique in their appearance and size, one of them then asked me if I would participate in lectures on Sarcoidosis. For a moment, I felt excited and important, the attention will feed my false ego with a false sense of purpose; now I would have a voice and be seen, and I never heard from them after that day. I am so happy it didn't manifest then, even though I wanted the publicity and (my ten minutes of fame) fanfare to feel important and thinking I would be doing the right thing for the good of others, the doctors would have played on my emotions, low self-esteem and ignorance by using me to perpetuate the disease, and thus, more people of color would have gotten this dis-ease really energy imbalance. .

"When we decide to stand tall, we really need to inner and over-stand what we are standing tall for."
-Rose Whaley

Over the years, while learning universal laws on the mental and emotional level and inner and over-standing how I manifested the dis-ease, I discovered the real unconscious core cause of all my conditions and how to prevent imbalances in my body. When someone you love dies (transition), the medical field and system plays on your grief or guilt, low self-esteem, and ignorance. They use your grief, pain or quilt for the purpose of starting up a memorial fund to get more money for the medical system and whatever foundation everyone is invested in for their profit. Instead of promoting the propaganda of unhealthiness, we should promote true healing and how to prevent the dis-eases. I went through a divine test with her church member after my Godmother's death's concerning the church collecting funds to put her name on a plague in her church, nobody will play on my emotions...I meant nobody...will use my love for my

30

love ones to get richer and continue misleading the masses in ignorance, fear and feeling of quilt for more greed and control!! If I didn't take heed to Benji's words or read the book he gave me, learning to apply the knowledge and wisdom, I would still be ill suffering unnecessarily, or maybe dead. I learned to go into my sanctuary, which in the bible is symbolic of the subconscious/ unconscious mind, and listen; not just hearing the CREATOR: your HIGHER SELF always sends the answers; we just keep missing them due to **ignorance** or **stupidity**. We can help change something that is wrong, imbalance or injustice to make a profound change in our life's and others. Self-reflect, meditate on this every day for at least nine or twenty-one days, and see what revelations are revealed about you, you know the song by MJ (the (person) in the mirror). Explore the following books and video to help you on your healing journey of true awakening: "African Holistic health" By Llaila O. Afrika, "Conquering Confusion" by Lorraine Day M.D., "The End of Disease" by David H. Fasliggi ScD., "Disease State of Consciousness" by Dr. Jewel Pookrum, Dr. SEBI- CURE for DIABETES, AIDS and CANCER.

"Let them alone, they are blind guides of the blind, and if a blind man guides a blind man, both will fall into a pit."
-Matthew 15:14

"Infinite intelligence knows the way out of any situation.   -Isaiah 43:19

"AGAIN"MOST PEOPLE ARE UNCONSCIOUSLY ADDICTED TO NEGATIVITY, PAIN, DRAMA AND ALL KIND OF SUFFERING.

THE FOUR O'S:

Omniscient - All knowing. Infinite knowledge and wisdom Divine mind is omniscient. It knows all.

Omnipotence - Infinite power. All the power there is. God is infinite power.

Omniscience - Having unlimited authority or influence; almighty.

Omnipresence - God is Mind. The one Mind contains all, and all ideas exist in the one Mind. God is everywhere present. There is no place God is not. She/he is in all divine creation, through all, and around all. Omnipresence is a spiritual realm that can be penetrated only through the most- highly accelerated mind/spirit action, as true prayer(is knowing it's done) and meditation. In the world today, there are thousands of humans that are walking encyclopedias and dictionaries that achieved all levels of academia in which they have accumulated a lot of data and so-called facts, all of which may be interesting; however, their personal lives are confused, mundane, and they are unconsciously unhappy. They have convinced themselves for so long, that they don't know the difference now. Some say that man is the sum total of his observable parts, which is absurd.

We are the temple of the Living God. We are more than our physical body, which is only an instrument used to reveal the Divinity within you.

SELF-HATRED is more OBVIOUS NOW THAN EVER! Look how most parents are publicly treating their children. What people are doing to themselves such as: men extreme muscle building, people tattooing and body piercing for no good reason, fingernails like animal's claws, permanent make-up cosmetic surgery, butt, breast (hmm) etc.? PEOPLE PAY TO HAVE PAIN INFLICED ON THEIR OWN BODY NOW FOR NO REAL REASON. -R.W.

Chapter 6
Illness (Disharmony)

I did not know then that the primary cause of most diseases, illnesses, pain, or accidents are due to mental and spiritual discord, and that some conditions are chosen (Dharma) by us before we reincarnate into the physical to provide universal lessons for individuals or humanity to be the example of prime creator power. In order to enjoy a permanent state of good health and true happiness, one must achieve and maintain mental and spiritual harmony. Now I over-stand that all the emotional and physical chaos I experienced was created in my mind, due to the low self-esteem and mental consciousness I had embraced.

When I was a young child in Georgia, I frequently used to experience extremely bad nosebleeds. I now know those nosebleeds were symptomatic of feeling unrecognized; they were my way of crying out for love, nurturing and attention. The tapeworms that consumed my body were manifestations of the victim state of consciousness I had embraced, a feeling that no one really cared for me. The asthma was symptomatic of my fear of life and the desire not to live in the bleak existence that I had ALLOWED to box me in. I am now aware that all the physical maladies and emotional unpleasantness I experienced were due to my self-hatred, criticism, prejudice, of self and inferiority that had dominated my sphere of not living my true DIVINE life.

The following is a list of more physical problems that plagued me early in my life and later, along with the unconscious feelings, beliefs, behavior, and/or attitudes that may have caused them. UN-Conscious affects every cell of your body, and every cell affects your consciousness.

Respiratory ailments (colds, congestion) – mental confusion, small hurts

Severe menstrual pain - guilt, fear

Hives and skin rashes - fear, anxiety, and feeling threatened

Migraine headaches - resisting the flow of life

Arthritis - feeling unloved, resentful, angry, fear of change and moving forward in life.

Hiatus hernias - feeling the burden of ruptured relationships

Lockjaw - anger, a refusal to express feelings

Lower back pains - feeling the fear of financial security and more.

Car sickness - feeling trapped

Yeast infections - denying my needs

Tonsillitis - swallowing negative emotions, such as anger, and refusing to change

Lung problems /Thyroid -depression, not feeling worthy of living your life fully

Nearsightedness - fear of seeing my future, addictions - fear, running from myself, not knowing how to love myself

Depression - anger, feeling powerless

Accidents - inability to speak up for self

Cold sores - festering anger, fear of expressing angry feelings

Constipation - refusing to release old ideas, patterns, programming, stuck in the past. Fever - anger, burning up inside.

My dear friend, **Ann Sealy** mailed me a great book, which confirmed some of the **imbalances in the body some of its causes,** and how you can heal. **I resonated with most of these conditions.** It is important to know that **health is the normal condition of your body.** True **healing is accepting and expressing the pure light of God.** Life does not get old or sick or diseased. Life is always whole, the **Divine Grace Life Force flows into you in the degree that you accept it.** Every person participates in some way in his or her physical problem. Of course, everyone also participates in his or her healing...or should. We need **FAITH WITH TRUST!**

John 3:16 - THE PRAYER OFFERED IN FAITH WILL SAVE THE ONE WHO IS SICK.

The need is to turn from attitudes and moods of negation that add up to a consciousness below the wellness-sustaining level which we might call "sickening," to a state of mind above that level, which **Dr. E. Butterworth** call "wholing." Wholing is what you do in terms of your **positive strategies for directing your mind and emotions in creative support of the Cosmic Healing Flow, which leads to wholeness. A few moments a day spent in consciousness** of wholing will ensure a symptom-free and disease-free life.

Dr. Reverend Eric Butterworth (from UNITY church)

Chapter 7

The Power of the Subconscious Mind

The subconscious mind is like a warehouse of memory. "As a man thinketh in is heart, so he is," (Proverbs 23:7) In other words, "You reap what you sow," "Cause and Effect," "Action causes Reaction," and "What goes around comes around." These all coincide with karma. Our UN or SUB- CONSCIOUS MIND ACCEPTS all habitual suggestions furnished by the conscious mind. It does not reason, rationalize, think, judge, balance, reject, or analyze any information or imagines that is submitted by the conscious mind. Like a computer, it accepts its program. Therefore all you heard, watch, think, feel, and believe is the cause of your habits; behavior and creation are the central mechanisms of your emotional, mental, physical, and spiritual well-being, It doesn't matter what religious dogma, label (box) you accept or ANYONE BOX.

According to Universal Laws, your UN- or SUB- CONSCIOUS MIND complies with the Law of Attraction, which states that everything housed in your subconscious mind for any length of time is brought into material existence by the power of your thoughts and strong feelings. Subconscious mind has the power and knowledge to heal, repair, destroy, or eliminate every disease, disharmony, or negative situation. Ignorance of the power of this level of consciousness was the cause of the discord I had previously experienced in my life and the disease that now invaded my body. When Spirit told me, "You asked for it," I wasn't willing to accept that truth because I didn't inner-stand the power of the subconscious mind. It wasn't until I finished reading The Key to yourself repeatedly until I inner/over-stood its principles that I realized, "Yes, I did ask for a disease in my ignorance that I thought was unfairly thrust upon me."

Entering the silence, by relaxing mind, body, spirit, and meditating every day, I learned to tap into my deeper mind. It vividly transported me back in time to when I was a girl around the tender age of nine, feeling unloved, neglected, unattractive, and inadequate. It was in Savannah, Georgia, during the 1950's, when color stratification was used as a powerful weapon for social, cultural and professional oppression and still today. If you weren't a light-complexioned individual with straight hair, your beauty and worth were ignored, and those in the African-American community who had such attributes were seen as the prize. Remnants of self-hatred, ingrained during centuries of slavery, still exist today in the psyche of majority of the African-American people.

Among my family members I witnessed favoritism toward my younger sister and others with fairer complexion and so-called good hair. Feeling they received more attention, a sense of unworthiness and unacceptability encroached upon my already deflated self-esteem. I grew up hating myself and feeling the need to be punished for my unacceptable looks by someone else's standards. I embraced victim consciousness and unknowingly created the conditions and circumstances necessary to bring about the disease and other imbalances. I did not realize I had the power to choose to create a healthy or unhealthy body, or that I could choose to be happy or unhappy, powerful or powerless, to feel beautiful or not, either choosing bravery or conformity. I NOW choose bravery! And it's very challenging.

The subconscious realm in man has twelve great centers of action. Each of these twelve centers has control over a certain function in the mind and body. The twelve centers are faith, strength, correct judgment, love, power, imagination, understanding, will, order, zeal, renunciation/elimination, and full life.

Negative consciousness - a mind filled with un-Godlike things, such as fear, hate, greed, lust, resentments, discouragement, sickness, and poverty.   -Charles Fillmore (page 42)

Negative consciousness - A mind filled with **un-Godlike things,** such as low self-esteem, always comparing, competing and judging, a fear of change, needing other **people's approval and acceptance**, feeling not good enough, jealousy, envy and vindictiveness and the list goes on   - **Rose Whaley**

The profound question is: What's in your Head (subconscious mind /heart) and not your wallet?

WHERE ARE OUR TRUE HEART, INTEGRITY, COURAGE, AND HUMANITY!!!

STILLNESS AND SILENCE IS ONE OF THE MOST IMPORTANCE PRACTICES WE MUST DO, TO COME OUT OF THE FIVE SENSES FREQUENCY RANGE.

AMERICA IS A CULTURE OF ENTERTAINMENT FOR MIND CONTROL, NOT FOR TRULY EVOLVING AND LIVING YOUR AUTHENTIC LIFE.

Chapter 8
The Healing Journey

Everything happens for a reason, in the beginning of my healing process, I met a new companion in 1988 named M. J. and he was gorgeous (hmm) I told him about the dis-ease, but he didn't say anything and asked me no questions about my condition. We never talked about it, either.

He planned a trip for us to go to Las Vegas in 1989. When we got off the airplane, I began to feel excruciating pain in my lungs, as if someone had my lungs in their hands squeezing the life force out of me. I could barely breathe. M. J. and the airport attendant tried to help me, but they didn't know what to do, touching or moving me in any way would cause more pain. I guided M. J. to look in my purse so he could retrieve the 800mg Motrin the doctors had prescribed, and the attendant gave me a cup of water. In about twenty minutes I was fine; MJ still asked me no questions.

Once I returned to New York City and he returned to Florida where he was living at the time, the relationship came to an abrupt end. I believed him when he expressed his love for me. Maybe he felt powerless seeing me in so much pain that day and couldn't and didn't know how to help me or maybe don't want to deal with it, thinking I would be in that condition always, or feared my health would worsen in time. Who really knows? After M. J. left my life, I focused more on learning to reconnect with my trueself. I believed M. J. and I had a true connection or maybe unconsciously I felt that way because he was an engineer for NASA and being with him then made me feel worthy. However, his departure assisted me in revealing the greatest love of all is and always was inside of me. Thank you, M. J. I thought it was you! (Everything happens for a DIVINE reason).

I have experienced some bad attacks several times in my apartment and once on the subway and had to be taken off the train and rushed to St. Barnabas Hospital's emergency room in the Bronx. I know now everything that happened was **strengthening, teaching, and preparing me to set an excellent example and become a powerful teacher,** to help people reclaim their **authentic self-power** and **natural state of wholeness.**

I had to be **willing to be wrong** in the **false limited beliefs that resided in me while awakening to truth and knowing was taking root.** The only way I could truly benefit from this extraordinary knowing was to **open myself fully to the universe in order to receive the healing that was** there, which is the force that **beats the heart within me (which resides in all of us).** The FORCE (GOD) words of wholeness, truth, love, strength, peace, guidance, wisdom, endurance and power are well-placed road maps for everyone's journey.

What are you doing to reconnect with all of yourself?

"I will instruct thee and teach in the way which thou should go; I will counsel you with my eye upon you. Do not be as the horse or the mule which have no understanding. Whose trapping include mouth bit and bridle to hold them in check. Otherwise, they will not come near you."
-Psalms 32:8-9

There is a guiding principle in all of us, an Infinite Intelligence that knows the answer and solution to every illusive problem.

Psalms 32:8 states this guidance and instruction is dependent on one having an understanding of the laws of the mind and the way of the Spirit, not consumed by man's law or religion. We are not like the horse and the mule, which are governed only by instinct and cannot reason critically like a man. Man, when he understands, can separate the chaff from the wheat, the false from the real.

Positive change is challenging, but you have the **choice. If you resist** change, you will pay a price sooner or later. It took me from three to perhaps as many as nine months of consciously working everyday on myself to form one new and better lifestyle habit, patterns, and actions to meet and accept my challenges for growth. Start small; there's wisdom in the saying, "One day at a time."

"Life is sometimes not easy, but it doesn't have to be hard."
-Rose Whaley

Disease - An inharmonious condition in mind and body brought by error thinking. **Ignorance causes all disease.** **"My people are destroyed for lack of knowledge"** (Hosea 4:6). Organic disease has its origin in mind as truly as any other manifestation. It has become subconscious and needs the power of the Christ Mind to reach and dissolve the error thoughts that are causing the disease -Charles Fillmore (page 55-56)

"There is no particular teaching. Teaching is in the moment. Words are like fog that one has to see through."
-Unknown

"Therefore, do not fear them, for there is nothing covered that will not be revealed and hidden that will not be known. What I tell you in the darkness, speak in the light; and what you hear whispered in your ear, proclaim upon the housetops" -Matthew 10:26-27

I am now aware and over-standing the importance of being still in the silence and meditating, listening to my soul, reciting prayers of thanksgiving to forgive myself and others, to send blessings of love to every divine creation in the universe. I am clearing my subconscious of all negative habits of worry, **all false fears and teachings about God,** myself and all life. I learned to clear, balance and open my chakras (energy centers in the etheric-body) everyday.

Etheric Body - Ether is a combination of all existing gases of nature. Your etheric body is energy equivalent to what we call spiritual beings.
-Rose Whaley

I gained knowledge of how to clear my aura, the energy field that surrounds our physical body, to take care of the physical body from the inside out, and so much more! I learned that getting a manicure or attaching fake nails, working out in a gym to develop the body, a new hairdo or hair weave, new designer clothes, cars, a home, jewelry, etc. (men you know what applies to you), working only on the outside, not realizing the most important aspect of the self is our consciousness, inner spirit and soul for SELF MASTERY. I started laying a spiritual foundation to keep my system clean by eating more live food, with higher energy life force; foods such as fruits and vegetables, especially green ones, drinking lots of water which I boil for ten minutes with a quartz crystal that I charge in the sun as long as possible then pour into a large glass container, juicing, drinking herbal tea, eliminating pork, beef, white rice, flour, sugar, dairy products, and sodas especially P. and C.C. (You know the drinks). I eliminated television shows, movies, gospel, songs, and other music that are vibrating on a low frequency of 440Hz etc. that doesn't empower the soul and have negative sublimed connotations to them. I'm exercising more in nature, leaning against trees, feet grounded in Mamma Earth and allowing her healing energy to come up through my feet, travel through my whole body, through the chakra centers, and then out of the crown chakra at the top of my head. I'm learning to just be still and know to take in everything nature has to offer: the sun, the moon, the sky, the stars, water, wind, fire, birds, as well as lower life forms.

Being truly connected, feeling oneness, peaceful, and a strong sense of being at home again, I love those moments. I am becoming more aware about what and who this force is we call God. God is everywhere if we choose to recognize this energy, and we are co-Creators with this force. We are all individual energy vibrating on different levels, creating a variety of experiences for different lessons to master in order to evolve back to God Consciousness (Then this game is over). Energy is the power of God within us to accomplish whatever we choose to manifest. Energy consists of atoms, molecules, photons, electrons, hydrogen etc., and the real Goddess/God self (the Universe).

TRUE COURAGE IS EMBRACING THE FEARS, LEARNING FROM IT AND WORKING THROUGH THE FEAR! -RW

LIST ONE OF YOUR FEARS! And WHY YOU FEAR IT.

Chapter 9
Renewing My Mind

After learning that I had mentally created the dis-ease invading my body I over-stood now that I could heal it by clearing my subconscious mind / heart and spirit of negative feeling, emotions, and replacing them with positive intentions, and loving thoughts to heal and stop resisting God's truth. Which required that I learn how to really love and be true myself and embracing my dark side which shows my unconscious true feelings, the area inside myself I need to continue working on to learn, heal and grow from, learning how to really love and forgive myself and others.

Letting go of resentment and anger, I conquered jealousy, low self-esteem, and releasing all kinds of fears by not being a co-dependent on any for my JOY. Most importantly, I had to take back my God-given power, my birthright. Being spiritual first and then accepting and owning my God given power. My first affirmation of many I would

utilize over and over in my journey back home.

I am God! God is as I am!

"I have said, ye are gods; and all of you are children of the Most High."
-Psalms 82:6

Here, the Bible explicitly tells us we are daughters and sons of the Infinite, and that the power of God is within us. We must know that we have inherited everything from Mother and Father God, and then we can grow in peace, wisdom, love, truth, and beauty. Through meditation and entering the silence, I gained direct knowledge and wisdom of who I am.

"There is no need for temples; no need for complicated philosophy. Our own heart is our temple; the philosophy is kindness."
- The 14th Dalai Lama of Tibet

I stopped believing in things without real knowledge, facts and inner/standing Instead, I inquiry, research, question, and study. Most of all I learned to go deeper in meditation which is listening to the most highest only; I especially stopped believing in institutionalized religion, spiritual or any false groups which are based on fear, blind obedience and false ego. They encourage the repression of real feelings, insisting it's virtuous to obey no matter what the content is which doesn't allow for the multitude of unique circumstances and conditions of each person. One had to fear God; you are not allowed to question the faith or their God. This was not true for me; I question God every day, debating, arguing, remembering, and laughing through it all now, I am creating my own relationship with that source most call God, known by many names! "Draw nearer to God, (not man,) and he will draw nearer to you."   -James 4:8

Repentance - Turning away from a belief in sin. Sin is thinking first in mind, or mental process. By going into the Silence, through meditation, error is brought into the light of Spirit (not man) and then transformed into a constructive force. Through the Christ mind, our sins (wrong thinking) are forgiven or pardoned (erased from consciousness). When we have cast all sins, error thoughts, out of mind, our body will be so pure that it cannot come under any supposed law of death or corruption. –C. Fillmore (167)

Check out: Dr. REV. RAY HIGINS - WHEN DID YOU STOP BEING A SLAVE, TO THE DARK ENTITIES, our shadow side.

"Be Ye transformed by the renewing of your mind Romans 12:2

The Three T's

Transformation - When we learn (remember) new concepts and know our true self - when we learn to let go of old forms and patterns - then we move into a new level of consciousness and into a new form.

Transmutation - means to really be changed, converted. When we get on the spiritual path, new forms appear. We acquire new friends. We have more love for everyone in the world, a greater sense of peace, abundance and freedom in our life, and the energy we once used to cause disease, aging, disharmony, depression, and other malfunctioned states is now repaired and transmuted to a higher vibration.

Transfiguration - supernatural change of appearance that takes place when one experiences the full flow of divine power through his/her own being.   -Rose Whaley

I learned (remember) how to reconnect to my sanctuary, my subconscious mind, "Upper room" (Act: 1:13), where the presence and power of God exists. I wasn't going to let false religious beliefs, dating back thousands of years (and now entrenched in the ideas and opinions of people today), govern my life. When I read in the Bible "The dead still rule," it's saying that the mind that molds our future through dead thoughts, ideas, and habitual conditions limits our evolution. Instead of using the word "Problem," I now use the word "Challenge." Challenges are a part of life, enabling us to learn our greatness and grow spiritually in order to realize who we really are and what our purpose is. "The dead praise not the lord, neither any that go down into silence" (Psalms 115:17). I was like the dead the Bible speaks of: those who do not know the laws of mind and of Infinite Spirit.   (a dead mind!).

After years of being conscious awakening by my own true inner Spirit, I learned how to accept and inner and over-stand all of life's painful experiences; opening me up to the real truth about God and myself (Know your **TRUE SELF, BEYOND THE BODY**), and know that true love is a powerful force. Being fearless, instead of hating, resenting, or fighting the dis-ease, I learned how to become one with it. I opened myself to the lessons it offered, and loved the disease away. **Continuing to learn and grow, thanking the universe everyday for that great opportunity that allowed me to really go deep in my subconscious mind, I had to be brave enough to step out of my comfort zone to seek true answers, because now, I had different questions.**

I stopped wearing long-sleeve tops and pants on the **hottest days of the summer, trying to hide the lesions;** there wasn't much I could do about the ones on my face. **Before having a shift in consciousness, I was unconsciously feeling like a victim, I didn't want people to stare or question me because they were afraid or thought I may have something contagious.** When someone did question me ("What's that on your face?"), **I mustered the courage to think and feel positive, not like a victim,** with confidence, faith, and trust in my higher-self, I replied with a smile, **"It's just a rash and it's going away!"** I didn't say, "My disease." To do so would have been giving the dis-ease power by claiming it. (You get it) **Instead of perpetuating the illness and believing the worse scenario for my future, I've learned how to use the same energies that I had used to create the disharmony in my mind, body, spirit and soul in order to heal. I used those energies to heal myself and be a source of light to help someone else who is ready to heal by facing all of their fears and painful feelings that are suppressed for many years.** I now over-stand the importance of reconnecting **(remembering) my whole self all aspect higher/lower/shadow etc. self my Goddess within.**

Energy cannot be destroy only transform.

"We are a temple of the living God."
-2 Corinthians 6:16

"Don't let the world around you squeeze you into its own mold, but let God remold your mind from within. Whatever you do, do your works heartily as for the lord rather than for men."   -
Colossians 3:23

The more in-tune I am with my inner God Consciousness the more I learned to listen not just with my ears, first with my heart, as well. Now I am able to **comprehend the true knowledge the universe is revealing to me every day,** and I am able to apply it to my life, getting the results I am seeking on all levels of my life. **Without human consciousness** there cannot be a human experience. We created the world we **have:** **99% followers, 1% true leaders. Monkey see, monkey do, and without any analyzing all concepts. Once the mass consciousness is seduced into ignorance by the mind controlling system with their false mainstream religious teachings, and with the system's propaganda with Materialistic, the mind is already conditioned. Now! Most people keep perpetuating their programming.**

It may vary here and there; however, **the concept is the same and they can easily capitalize on the mind of most people who are not aware of the whole truth! I used creative visualization** and imagination until **I got what I felt, claimed and affirmed everyday! Forming a mental picture in my mind's eye (third eye chakra), I envisioned the doctor examining me and checking the x-rays of my lungs. I saw, heard, and felt her telling me that my lungs were all clear, and that they looked like there had never been anything wrong with them. I was exhilarated when she said those words. Faith is evident of the unseen; truth reveals itself sooner or later, what are you creating right now!**

48

I continued enduring the painful and challenging spiritual work within myself; feeling assured that everything would unfold and be fine better than ever. I started missing some of my monthly treatments, and the doctor commented that I wasn't taking the disease seriously. My reply was, "It's not anymore!" **I came out of that energetic timeline.** To help change something that is wrong or injustice, and make a profound change in our life and the life of others. **Self-reflect, meditate on this every day for at least nine or twenty-one days, and see what revelations are revealed to you.**

"He sent his word and healed them and delivered them from their destruction   -Psalms 107:20"

Cease striving, and know I am God"   -Psalms 46:10

Consciousness - The sense of awareness, of knowing, the knowledge or realization of any idea, object, or condition. The sum total of all ideas accumulated in and affecting man's present being. Composite of ideas, thoughts, emotions, sensation and knowledge that makes up the conscious, subconscious, and **super-conscious phases of mind.** It includes all that man is aware of - spirit, soul, and body. It's very important to inner-stand the importance of our consciousness for spiritual growth. **Divine ideas must be incorporated into our consciousness before they can mean anything to us.** An intellectual concept does not suffice. **To be satisfied with an intellectual understanding leaves us subject to sin, sickness, poverty, and death. To assure continuity of spirit, soul, and body as a whole, we must ever seek to incorporate divine ideas into our mind. A consciousness of eternal life places one in the stream of life that never fails.** C. F. (page 41)

Visualize - means to recall something you have seen, felt, or experienced visible in your mind's eye, feeling it in your heart, your whole body (every cells).

Imagination - is to imagine something you've never seen or felt that hasn't happened yet. Imagine in your mind's eye, feeling it in your heart, and in your whole body. Every cell of your body has a consciousness, and it can't tell the difference between what you imagine whether, is true or not. -R.W.

"Imagination is more important than knowledge.
A. E.

Poem:
EYE OF THE SOUL
I learned to close my eyes so that I can see! "Thanks, Divine Creator, for my single (third) eye. It's the wisdom of my heart/soul. It helps me to see within my true self and all that I behold as true. Dear Lord grant me the wisdom to determine reality from illusions. Grant me the strength and courage that I may keep evolving spiritually. Help me to stay focus only on your good, love and beauty, and with my eye within, let my focus stay on your truth within my COSMIC SELF. Thank you, Infinite Intelligence. -R.W.

Chapter 10
Trusting True Spirit

In the spring of 1994, I reached for my medication, which I kept on top of the refrigerator. Taking medication was something I had become accustomed to doing on a daily basis since my medical diagnosis. This day, as I held the pill in my hand ready to consume it my inner Spirit said, **"You don't need to take the medication anymore.** You are healed." **I hesitated in putting the medication back and felt confused, as new sores** were becoming visible on my skin. In choosing to trust Spirit, I **was willing to risk whatever side effects might result in my complete withdrawal from my oral medication.** Choosing to obey my internal guide, I was now walking in faith. I was **secure in my choice** due to all of the **previously experiences that had enlightened me on my conscious spiritual journey,** which was a total of maybe seven years. If there was anything I was certain of, it was that CREATOR had never let me down. **I surrendered my decision unto the Creator within my HEART.**

September 1994, I opened **my second custom made fashion boutique on Fordham Road in the Bronx.** In October, my friend **Luisa** visited me and while we were conversing all of a sudden, she stared at my face and asked, "When did the lesions disappear from your face?"

I was amazed by her inquiry, because being at one with the healing, I no longer gave the illness any power, and realizing true faith and trust, I had **completely forgotten about the lesions.** I ran quickly to a mirror and a **wave of astonishment greeted me when viewing the clarity of my face.** Immediately a rush of love and a sense of freedom engulfed me. **Thanking the universe** for its great laws of truth and power of the mind, my beliefs in faith continued to grow stronger because truth always reveals itself. **IT IN YOUR SUPER CONSCIOUS NESS!!!**

About two weeks later, the still soft voice said, "Schedule an appointment to see the **gynecologist** to have your birth control device removed." (**The birth control device** was called (**Copper Seven.**) I was surprised to get this message, because for years the device had never given me any problems. **Yet, it was another example of the journey to listening, and obeying my true Spirit was continuous.** Weeks later I was at the clinic insisting that the doctor remove the device. After the examination he too, was baffled by my decision **to remove the Copper Seven since everything looked good.** Can you imagine me telling the doctor my Spirit told me to have the device removed, especially in **1994!** Finally he informed me that they no longer removed the devices in the clinic. **He said several tests and a chest x-ray had to be performed first before the procedure would be allowed, which required a one-day hospital stay.** I knew the issue was about getting paid; they knew I had Medicaid. (HA!) Once the procedure was done and the anesthesia wore off in the recovery room this attractive, pleasant, black female doctor asked me, "How are you feeling?" I responded **"Fine" she noticed the lesions on my arms. "What is that?"** she asked the look on her face and the tone in her voice made me think she thought I was a drug user or was **HIV positive.** I replied, **"I had** Sarcoidosis." (**An energy imbalance**) She then said, "You couldn't **have had that disease. I checked your x-ray, and your lungs are sparkling clear.**" Those words were a **burst of exhilaration to my heart,** mind, and ears. Every cell in my body felt like they were singing a happy tune. **My faith and trust was confirmed. My cup runneth over with joy now!**

Faith, center of - **The pineal gland, located in the middle of the brain,** is the center of faith in the body of man. **Concentration** of thought on this center opens the mind of man to **spiritual faith** –C. Fillmore (page 68)

Faith in oneself - The ground for **man's faith** in him or herself is the truth that he/she is a child of God and, as such, **inherits Divine Nature.** We should have faith in our self because without it, we cannot be successful at anything.   -Charles Fillmore (page 69)

I learned (remembered) how to just be still and go into the silence, and tithe every day. That 10% to Melchizedek refers to the "I AM" or "presence of God in you," not a book or building, not 10% of your income! The book of Genesis talks about Melchizedek, which is not a physical person. It's who most westerners refer to as Jesus. Melchizedek is a symbolic representation of the dark matter that makes up 90% of the universe (the right side of the brain). That is why it requires 10% from us in meditation. You can find more information regarding Melchizedek online at www.hiddenmeanings.com.

"I have many more things to say to you, but you cannot hear them now. The Spirit of truth comes. He will guide you into all the truth; for he will not speak on his own initiative, but whatever he hears, he will speak; and he will disclose to you what is to come." -John 16:12-13

A priest in Biblical language is a mediator between the Invisible presence and the Visible. It doesn't refer to a **physical man.** It is your state of mind and **raising our vibration frequency** to real truth and power within self that brings you out of your misery, your pain or limitation, and mediates between the two states.

We are taught that in the end we will be judged and condemned by the Creator for our sins. The truth is we are reaping what we sow in our present life or a past life. That's the real judgment. That's why most of us experience so much unhappiness, pain, and illnesses of all kinds because of our false beliefs, negative thinking, and feelings. Most victims Consciousness is created when we allow the main media and religions or other groups to convince us that something is wrong with us as THE CREATOR (God) created us.

People convince us that we need to be part of some institutionalized false spirituality religious group and with materialism, using reverse psychology, which allows someone else to control your thinking and life, like with (THE AMERICAN DREAM?) WHAT'S YOUR DIVINE DREAM OR VISION/ MISSION?

They don't have to worry about what you would think, say and do; they already know your thought process.

"MIND CONTROL" LIKE ROBOTS, LOOK WHAT MOST EVERYONE ARE BELIEVING IN, WATCHING, READING, LISTENING TO NEGATIVE AND DIS-EMPOWERING THINGS AND CONSTANTLY WEARING AND BUYING THE SAME FASHION STYLES, CARS, JEWELRY ETC.,THE AMERICA SO CALL DREAM TO FIT IN TO GET APPROVAL FROM WHO?(NOT FROM PRIME CREATOR/GOD!)

SHEEPS FOLLOWERS, NOT LIONS/LEADER

Chapter 11
True Faith Is Knowing, Not Believing

"O you of little faith, why did you doubt." - Matthew 14:31

I am very happy that I trusted this Infinite Intelligence we call God. Spirit revealed to me a few weeks before the procedure that I was healed and no longer needed to continue taking the pills. Even though new lesions were manifesting on my skin, **I obeyed and trusted the Spirit of Prime Creator/God, and that day in Union Hospital in the Bronx**, I got my confirmation. **Trusting** in the God/ CREATOR/ is the beginning of true wisdom and divine power.

"For great is thy mercy toward me, and thou has delivered my soul from the lowest of hell."   -Psalms 86:13

Hell - meaning bondage, restriction, fear, illness, pain, suffering of all kind, etc., most of which are all self-imposed, due to ignorance or false concepts of God (ourselves). We keep allowing the system, religion, and other people to control our minds.   -Rose W. Williams

When I went back to my original doctor at St. Barnabas Hospital and expressed with joy that I was healed, the doctor insisted I have another chest x-ray done (you know doctors), I did and the healing was confirmed again! They wanted me to come back in a few months to have another x-ray they never seen me again.

Whatever you continuously listen to and impress in your un/subconscious mind, will come forth and be objectified and experienced by you.

It doesn't matter whether you're a Christian, Muslim, Seventh Day Adventist, Catholic, a Jew, Protestant, Buddhist, Baptist, Hindu, Jehovah's Witness, Atheist or whether you're a so-called good or bad person.

(Timothy 4:1-2) Spirit explicitly says that in later times some will fall away from the faith, paying attention to deceitful Spirits and doctrines of demons by means of the hypocrisy of liars seared in their own conscience as with a branding iron. It depends on your growth lessons, challenges, and what your **SOUL** came here to experience for its next level to evolve. , It's about what your soul came here to change, to make greater for **all humanity**. It's about a shift in consciousness and raising that consciousness to higher vibrations, **back to God (UNITY) consciousness.**

Cause and Effect – The law of sequence; the balance wheel of the universe, this law, like all other divine laws, inheres in all divine **being it must be a balance.** "**Whatsoever a man soweth, that shall he also reap**" (Galatians 6:7). Man lives in two worlds, the world of cause (the within) and the world of effect the without.-C.F.pg.31

I didn't just heal the disease; I started facing most of my fears, low self-esteem, and worked through them and no more arthritis, migraines, emotional allergies, female problems, bad eyesight, and hiatus hernias. Now I feel great, powerful, healthy, stronger, young, and pain free! Most of all, I freed my mind from servitude to anyone other than the true Source. **Truth will set you free! The Christ said, "Your faith has healed you."** Who and what do you really have faith in? Man (**dark entities**) or the **true God Spirit within you?** I didn't just learn (remember) how to heal myself, but got at the core cause of all the **disharmonies. First, I had to recognize that within me is a power greater (unseen) than what is in front of me.** My newest daily

56

affirmation is, "Everything in my life is in Divine Order. Spirit helps me to see through the illusions and to know that I have the strength and courage to endure any experience, to recognize and inner/overstand all lessons to continue learning and growing spiritually in order to remain spiritually whole. Thank you, "Divine Spirit."

Are you being asked to risk reaching out to ask for help now? Are you being asked to make a leap of faith into an uncertain future? The greatest rewards for our challenges in life are not what we get from it, such as material gains, but by becoming what we were created to be... powerful, joyous, loving, giving, wise "Children of the PRIME CREATOR (GOD)."

"For where your treasure (thought) is, there will your heart be also."
-Luke 12:33(HEART represents the SUBCONSCIOUS MIND.)
Suffering is not necessary for our development; it is the result of violations of the DIVINE SPIRITUAL LAWS. You can have a condition and not suffer.

UNPLUG FROM THIS FALSE CONSTRUCT OF CONFORMITY AND MIND CONTROL and CLEANSE AND RE-OPEN YOUR HEART CENTER!

"If your eye be single, your whole body will be full of light." Truth! –Matt. 6:22

Chapter 12
Truth Reveals Itself

On a bright and warm Thursday in **March of 1998**, I began to feel severe pain on the right side **(kidney area)** of my body and extreme pressure in my head at that time; **I hadn't had a headache in about a year.** Feeling that something was seriously wrong, I considered going to the hospital, but when my inner Spirit said, "If you go to the hospital, they will admit you." I continued going about my day, doing household chores and **ignoring the signals my body was sending me.**

That evening, my companion, Ernest, came to visit me, and sensed something was wrong with me, **he felt compelled to check my forehead for any sign of a fever.** Although I didn't feel like I have a fever from the outside, **he insisted that I be examine by a doctor.** I refused because I was facilitating a spiritual workshop in my apartment that Sunday and didn't want to cancel it. I love what I do for Prime Creator!!!

I later realized it was another opportunity to learn, grow, and strengthen my faith in HIGHER DIVINE FREQUENCY. I got quiet and went within myself, **asking Spirit to help me get through the weekend and my workshop then I would go to the hospital afterward.** I wasn't worried or fearful about the condition of my body after **surrendering.** A sense of peace came over me.

"I did not give you a spirit of fear. I gave you love, a sound mind and power."
-2 Timothy 1:7-8

Chapter 13
Countdown

Friday, the second day, I was still **feeling pain and pressure in my head,** but I **still chose to ignore it** and continue with my household chores. That evening, internally my body felt like an iceberg something I have never experienced before. Shortly **I through my body temperature had dropped I felt like I was freezing I started shaking for about a half hour.** I took a hot shower trying to warm my body, it didn't work. Later that evening, my youngest son, **Clifford (known by his spiritual name SHINE)** came home and knew something was wrong because I was in bed too early; usually **I am a nocturnal individual who works until the wee hours of the morning.** He realized **I was sick;** he also tried to convince me to go to the hospital. I said, **"No! I'll be alright."** He put more blankets on me and wrapped his arms around me trying to warm my body. **Finally I fell asleep.**

Saturday, the third day, I felt the same while food shopping, cleaning the apartment, and preparing for the Sunday afternoon spiritual healing and empowering workshop. **That evening my body began to freeze and shake again for about a half hour again,** I took a hot shower and then lay on the couch in the living room, covered myself with a blankets. **Once again my son Shine came home to find me already retired for the evening, he woke me up to suggest I get in my bed because I was in the living room on the sofa near an open window. He pulled the blankets off me to discover I was soaked in my own sweat; it was as if someone had poured gallons of water on me, internally I felt good and like my whole body was on fire.** I can't really explain it, but something **powerful was happening inside of me. I felt a release.** Now I inner/over-stand from reading the book- **Songs of God that what I was experiencing was the wrath of God (Spirit), a great Spiritual intervention that precedes the healing of any condition.**

59

Wrath, of God – Meta - Some Bible authorities claim that the "wrath of God," or of the Lord (Romans 1:18), might with equal propriety be translated the "blessing" of the Lord. We know that after the destruction of limited and inferior thoughts and forms of life, other and higher thoughts and forms take their place, and the change is actually a blessing in the end. So even the "wrath" that comes to our fleshly tabernacles, when we persist in holding them in material thought, is a blessing ultimately. When we are loving and nonresistant, we do not suffer under the transformations that go on when the Mosaic Law is being carried out. The "wrath of God" is really the working out of the Law of being destructively or in harmoniously for the individual who does not conform to the law, but thinks and acts in opposition to it. - Metaphysical Bible Dictionary by Unity (page 681)

The fourth day, Sunday I felt much better, It was a bright, sunny day. My companion and I went to a flea market in Queens that morning. We walked around for a few hours while the sun was beaming down on my whole being, which felt great to me since I love the sun now. Ernest was still concerned about my health since he noticed my hand occasionally resting on my right side. He asked me how I was feeling; I told him I felt fine, even though there was still a little discomfort.

We returned to my apartment and set up the room for the workshop. Instead of the scheduled two hours, it lasted over six hours. I didn't tell anyone I wasn't feeling good, I wasn't as talkative as usual; and anyone who know me, knows I can talk for hours, when it's of true significant, something that can really help people, help themselves. After the workshop was over and everyone had left, I took a shower thanking the Creator for grace, helping me through that weekend. When Monday arrived, I kept my agreement, and went to Montefiore Hospital's emergency room and relayed my symptoms to the nurse. She took my temperature to my surprise it was 103. Next thing I knew,

I was in a hospital bed with an IV in my arm and doctors hovering around me asking all kinds of questions, such as "How long have you been feeling ill? "Are you able to eat?" "Are you dizzy?" "Do you have blurred vision?" "Are you feeling weak?" and "Have you passed out recently?" "No, no, no!" I exclaimed. "What is wrong with me?"

Still not receiving a prognosis, they proceeded with blood testing then said they couldn't believe I didn't have any other symptoms. They looked very puzzled. They left my bedside, then came back and asked me more questions. Finally, the doctor told me I had a kidney infection that had gone through all the stages which was critical and my blood test was evident. The high fever had caused convulsions and my eradicate temperature swings, but what the physicians couldn't understand how I was able to functioned for the four days without medical treatment. The doctor said I had come to the hospital when the worst was already over; my immune system had kicked in, destroying the infection. The doctor informed me that I had a healthy body and a strong immune system. From what I inner and over-stand from reading the book-Songs of God by J. Murphy, my temperature rose so high in order to kill the virulent bacteria causing the infection I didn't know I had.

They then asked me what special way I took care of myself. I told them that I meditate every day, practice forgiveness and positive thinking, extended kindness to myself and others drink lots of good water, juiced, and I ate healthier foods and most importantly, I made an effort to listen to and trust my own body and true spirit. Their response was, "Keep doing what you're doing."

That evening, I was discharged with a prescription for penicillin, which I didn't take because my body and Spirit told me I didn't need it. Learning and inner/over-standing our bodies are very important. No one should know your body better than you. Spirit is always on time, my Medicaid expired the next day, and it wasn't going to be renewed. When I fully realized and over-stood the whole process of what the experience taught me, I experienced a resurrection. I am now vibrating at a higher level of consciousness.

The whole universe is vibrating and works according to Universal Laws. Each particular thing or person has its own rate of vibration.

Vibration, Thought - Energy sent out by the power of thought (your thoughts).   -Charles Fillmore (page 205)

Resurrection - The restoring of mind and body to their original, undying state. This is accomplished by realization that God is Spirit and that God created man with power like that which He Himself possesses. When man realizes this mind and body automatically become immortal.   -Charles Fillmore (page 169)

Faith of Understanding - Faith that functions from Principle. It is based on knowledge of Truth. It understands the law of mind action; therefore, it has great strength. To know that certain causes produce certain results gives a bedrock foundation for faith. -C.Fillmore (page 70)

God as Health - God is absolute wholeness and perfection. Man's recognition of his oneness with this perfect wholeness through Christ brings him into the consciousness of his indwelling life and health. "I in them, and thou in me, that they may be perfected into one" -Charles Fillmore (page 83)   and (Read John 17:

Chapter 14
Courage To Heal

"There is an answer to every challenge (problem), and healing wisdom is in the challenge."   -Rose Whaley

About a week later, I took my **daughter Adrienne** to see my **mentor Susie** for a spiritual message. The best! I waited for her in Susie meditation room; her whole house is very peaceful, loving, and beautiful to me. **Susie** put on a videotape for me to watch. The title was **"Workshop in Spirituality: "Focus on the Chakras"** by **Dr. Budri Richi,** as I watched and listened, **Dr. Richi started explaining the energy centers (chakras)** in the **etheric bodies.**

An etheric body is the combination of all existing gases of nature. It is an energy body we call the "spiritual being." It explains how the glands and emotions are related to a particular center, **what illnesses are related to that center, and how our negative thoughts, feelings, and fears can manifest a specific pain, illness, or "accident."**

While **Dr. Richi** was explaining **the second chakra**, the one at the **lower abdominal area,** the color for that center is orange, and it is the center for **procreation, physical force, vitality,** etc. **I realized that my energy there (the sacral plexus) was channeled in a negative way, due to my fear of writing this book because of my lack of a formal education and feelings of inadequacy, unqualified and fear of how people will perceive me and my work.**

I wasn't feeling these emotions on a conscious level, but on a subconscious or unconscious level, not knowing those feelings caused the manifestation of the kidney condition.

For years, I have been writing and stopping, never completing it until now, after years of experiencing the kidney infection, when I stopped focusing on completing this book. I sometimes experienced a little pain in that same area as a reminder to do what true Spirit wanted me to do (My Soul Mission) in spite of my fears of my capability and what people would think of me. .

"If I be lifted up from the earth, will draw men unto me; when you lift up your ideas or desires to the point of acceptance in your mind, your prayers will be answered and you will bring forth the manifestation."   -John 12:32-36

YOU ARE A CO- CREATOR! Make Something Divine and Great Happen Now, CREATE A BETTER YOU and WORLD!

WHY ARE YOU AFRAID TO UNPLUG FROM THIS NEGATIVE MATRIX OF CONTROL?

DO NOT DIE (leaving here) JUST BECAUSE, BUT FOR A DIVINE CAUSE!

-RW.

GO BEYOND THE MIND!

Chapter 15
One's Purpose on Earth

My purpose on Earth at this time is to help raise the consciousness of those who are ready to face false fears and illusions that have ENSLAVED their minds and SOUL /HEART; illusions which have allowed them to be controlled for generations. My purpose is also to assist these individuals in knowing and using their God-given power righteously for the good of all. Nothing should matter to you more than knowing your true Soul's purpose for your life, and nothing can compensate for you not knowing. We were created by God (pure energy), in order for God to experience itself through us, we must start with self, not with man's lust for material gains or his religious or political pursuits for World domination. Now that I know my true purpose, I have a responsibility to all life. If I do not continue the pursuit of my Soul purpose, I will cease living, because there will be no real purpose for me to be here. I surrendered myself to the Creator to be used for its purpose (righteousness), not mine. Most people have abandoned living for God's great purpose by choosing a false sense of personal fulfillment with the pursuit of material goods and religious dogma.

"Do you not know that when you present yourself to someone as slaves for obedience, you are slaves of the one whom you obey, either of sin resulting in death or of obedience resulting in righteousness -Romans 6:16

"Do not reject the spiritual gift within you, which was bestowed upon you through prophetic utterance with the laying on of hands by the presbytery. Take pain with these things; be absorbed in them, so that your progress may be evident to all."   -1: Timothy 4:14-15

"You did not choose me, I chose you and appointed you that you should go and bear fruit." (Express God's love and power).   -John 15:16

We are all unique and came here to Earth not to conform and follow an old trail, but to evolve and leave a new trail of awareness. I went seeking a cure and found (reconnected to) the key to everything. God (within)! Seek and you will find. I am and you are a co-Creator of the true Spirit within.   **I love you all! Peace!**

"If you make people think they are thinking for themselves, they will love and admire you. But if you really make them think, they will hate or despise you." -Unknown

"We fear things we think we are not aware of. We deny and fight against things we think we don't understand" -RW

LEARNING TO REMEMBER!

Chapter 16
Lost Soul

I am writing at this present moment, **April 2005, my father, Corrie Lee Williams**, has been living at the Daughters of Jacobi Rehabilitation Center in the Bronx for about a year now. He is suffering from a debilitating form of **rheumatoid arthritis and can't bend his fingers; he has to use a wheelchair.** That same year and the year before, he had two operations, one for prostate cancer and the other was a kidney problem, only to **prolong his agony.** (I look at his life and ask myself for what?) I don't really like visiting him, because he looks sad and thin like a skeleton wearing a Pamper. **His Spirit and will had been broken a long time ago by this mentally ill sick society,** and is like so many people **just going through the motions of so-called living, letting others mold them, feeling no real value or sense of Soul purpose.** They don't really know how to truly be honest and love themselves first and others, or how to receive **unconditional love or any kind of love.**

At the age of seventy-five, he still allowed himself to stay stuck in this deeper hole, because of his false fears, inferiority, and ignorance; therefore, settling for a limited existence. I would not let him or anyone else make me feel guilty are obligated for his condition. I felt that his Spirit was ready to go back home to regroup and to re-incarnate in order to try this physical experience again to grow, learn (remember) to do it better the next re-incarnation life experience. **February 18, 2005, I** was at **Bronxnet cable studio** dubbing **some tapes for a few hours,** when I **simultaneously** felt inspired to write about my Dad. **I tried to recall my earlier childhood memories of him, to my amazement, I couldn't remember anything positive.** There was an inability to see him visibly or feel him in my heart. Although the **memory of my parents' excessive drinking and constant fighting rushed to the forefront of my memory, I still couldn't visualize my father in the earlier years of my life. Knowing we were in the same household,** yet being unable to feel him left me with a deep feeling **of emptiness inside.** There was **no real bonding, nurturing, support, or guidance from him of any kind.** I feel like I never had what we consider a real father. **I became a mother at fifteen, got married at sixteen and moved out of my parents' home.** Today, **I realize I really don't know this man I call "Daddy", and he really doesn't know me and shows no real interest of finding out whom I am, but I over-stand why.** It's about him not been taught (reminded) to believe and know his **true God-self,** which allows him to be **stuck in ignorance** and **victim consciousness** that allows this system **to implant a false Spirit of fear, guilt, unworthiness, and powerlessness.**

Having a strong urge to just be with him, **I left BRONXNET** and went straight over to the **rehabilitation center** to see him. I wanted to look at him with new eyes, to see what was really there and not just what I wanted to see. **He was surprised to see me because I didn't visit everyday, (because I didn't want to)** when he opened his eyes and saw me standing at his bedside, his eyes lit up. **This was significant because he could never look me directly in the eyes.** I helped him out of the bed, into the wheelchair, **I pushed him in the corridor** by the window where **the sun was shining bright, feeling warm, peaceful, and beautiful.** I felt it rays begin healing both of us **with unconditional love.**

He talked about frivolous things in the beginning of our visit. Then gradually he began to open up, discussing how **he felt like a failure and was hurting from feelings of shame, guilt, unworthiness, and that he never knew what his real purpose was in his lifetime.** When he shared some of the painful events in his childhood, **I discovered that his father was killed when he was about six years old,** working in the **sugar cane** field **he got caught in the machine that grinds up the cane and was mangled. That loss was compounded when his mother died of cancer when he was nine years old.** Disclosing these **unknown facts** to me for

68

the first time, tears swelled in his eyes and the sadness in his voice was undeniable - his pain was still present in his unconscious.

I can only imagine what it feels like for him. I don't want to just say I love him out of obligation; I wanted to really tap into that true love within myself for him that the CREATOR put inside of all of us. I was eager to put my arms around him, just to hold him and cry for the both of us, but he resisted my affections as always. No hugging, kissing, or touching. He was still afraid to show or receive affection which is under-stand able.

A couple of years before his body totally shut down, I made the effort to create a bond by taking him to Atlantic City on "Father's Day" and it was starting to work. He enjoyed the bus ride, being on the Boardwalk, and watching the outside activities. We missed our times together! I realized I felt deprived of my dad again, and was angry because of his condition, behind anger is really hurt!

Another reason I didn't like visiting him, I felt and witness so much sadness and pain in the eyes of the many patients that were aligned in the corridors with disease (Disharmony), such as obesity, catatonic states of mind, hooked to machines and tubes, incoherent patients, amputated limbs, their clothing soiled with defecation...just all kinds of physical, mental, and spiritual disharmony. It's not a pretty sight.

When entering my dad's room, I noticed his roommate lying in his bed with the sheet pulled over his head. I was shocked seeing only the top part of his body, but where was the rest of his body? I asked my father about him, he told me that he lost his lower body to diabetes and that no one had come to visit him in over a year now. He acted mean, nasty, and never smile. I wonder what he is really feels about his life and what kind of person he was to end up like this feeling negative and

69

anger, behind anger is feeling of hurt. He doesn't seem to have learned the lessons either. His situation instantly makes me think of the Universal Law "You reap what you sow." Being there feels like I am in a living graveyard, bodies walking around, but spiritually dead. I telepathically blessed them sending light and love energy to all of them.

At the center I observe the unhealthy and overcooked foods being served with no real nutrients or life energy (Chi) for healing and restoring the body back to its natural state. My mother and other siblings contribute to my father's poor diet out of their ignorance or didn't really cared by bringing more unhealthy foods, Pepsi, Coke Cola and junk foods. Now, he will not eat soup without putting plenty of white sugar in it. He didn't listen to me. (He made his transition in 2006)

In all of his seventy-five years, he never believed in religion or church. Now that he's in the center feeling desperate and at his lowest emotionally, he attends a church service in the center and is talking about Pope John Paul II transition (death) after his highly televised. He talks about how good he thinks the Pope was, and what he had to say sounded right and good. I laughed and said, "They've suckered you in too, with their seductive and deceptive subliminal messages; much like the pimps and con artists who work earnestly at weaving and convincing of their good intentions." I told him the Pope was on television in 1999 saying, "Hell is a state of mind," and what amazed me is that every religious person I spoke to said they didn't see or heard he relayed that message. However, they were fully exposed via news coverage or word of mouth about the Michael Jackson and Kobe Bryant trials. Let me end this train of thought because this is another book altogether!

I realized, he was unconsciously using his unhealthy body condition which he has manifested over the years, to justify him not doing anything **profound,** his SOUL PURPOSE for his life. **By not taking full responsibility and resisting change in his life, his body completely shut down because he totally gave up on his self on all levels,** he doesn't have to really do anything now, and being in that condition gives him **another excuse and a sense of false value to get attention.** He naively believes all the people working there really care about him some of them did care, **but most hmm; to them it's just about getting paid like most churches and politicians.**

"Do not love the world or the things in the world; if anyone loves the world, the love of the father is not in him. For all that is in the world, the lust of the flesh and the lust of the eyes and the boastful pride of life, is not from the father, but is from the world and the world is passing away and also its lust, but the one who does the will of God abides forever." -1 John 2:15-17

When my siblings and I were growing up in the South, our parents didn't choose **false religion** or **the American Dream** to ESCAPE their false insecurities, deficiencies, inferiority, fears, unhappiness, ignorance and pain. They chose partying, drinking, gambling, smoking, infidelity, and fighting with each other; unfortunately, they didn't understand they were hurting and demanding their children the ones they were supposed to love. This train of thought will be continued in another book. **My father asks** me all of the time to tell **certain people** that he is there and to come see him. My reply was, **"What's your point? (Emotional victim Consciousness pays off) Those people didn't call or come see you in years when you were home and walking around."** I knew it was about the pity party feeling PITY is LOVE. And to feel important, to get attention for feeling powerless and purposeless and I had a neighbor next door, and for over twenty years, all I have gotten from her is just a hello or goodbye in passing. One day she invited me to her apartment door, but I saw beyond the door and wondered how she could live in an apartment filled with so much clutter. I mean soooo much junk! She never opened the windows or raised her shades. This was around 1990 she shared some of her unhealthy issues which was a lot. Since I have known her, she has always been obese; this **affected her breathing and walking**. I suggested some things she could do to restore her health and gave her a cassette tape on the **Laws of Attraction**, which explains **why we get what we get and how to reverse it if we choose to,** but she never listened, questioned, or talked to me about it anymore. Hum! **I moved across the street in 1998,** I still see her walking with a cane once in a while on the hottest days during the summer, **wearing winter clothing from head to toe, sweating like she was in a sauna.**

2003, I heard a knock on my door. Upon opening it, she was standing before me **looking happy and excited** for the first time since I've known her. She just wanted to introduce me to her **caretaker** whom job was to take care of her. **(Do you get the picture?) Paying attention to myself first and other people's disharmony or their KARMA** makes me more appreciative of my whole body, especially my lungs and skin. Because of the **Sarcoidosis,** I've learned the importance of **breathing properly, a cleaner environment, using the natural Aloe Vera plant and others, instead of chemical creams on my skin, body piercing or tattooing is a no, no! Karma is a serious!** I visit my father more frequently...**not out of obligation or feeling guilty, but to develop my love for him, knowing deep inside his love for me is there, too. No one taught him how to reconnect to his love and bring it out, or how to develop a real bond in a positive, nurturing way. It's challenging to show someone love, who is afraid of love and doesn't know how to really show or receive it.** He still has a good sense of humor and flirts with the female employees. **He has this funny look in his eyes and look on his face that still makes me smile.** He still likes to make jokes like, "Where's my drink," or "Give me some of what you're drinking," **insinuating that it is booze,** he use to **abused booze**. The employees really seem to like him because he is **very grateful and does not hesitate to show his appreciation by saying, "Thank you."** He even thanked me for coming to see him. Dad, **I am making more of an effort to feel that true love for you that I know is deep inside of me.** I just need to go through my healing process in order to connect too. **Thank you for being my Father,** for opening my mind and heart in order to seek the true knowledge and wisdom of inner and over-standing **unconditional love, faith, endurance, compassion, courage, detachment and most of all to know my true Goddess self.** You lost your way, and in the process, helped me to **realize my true-self and Soul purpose path.**

The weekend of **October 8, 2005** was the first time I got my dad from the rehabilitation home, wheelchair and all, which he had been in for the last two years to spend the weekend with me at my apartment. There were **all kinds of obstacles in my way on the day** I picked him up. However, I didn't let it discourage me or thinking that having him with me would be too hard.

When I surrender the situation into the hands of the PRIME Creator/GOD, it was an easy and wonderful weekend. I even took him over to his own apartment, which made him even happier; he hadn't been there in about two years, **believing he couldn't walk up three flights of stairs. I didn't allow him to play the victim,** I stood behind him just in case he loses his balance, **and he did it within twenty minutes.** The pets he loves did not **acknowledge him,** which hurt him, I told him to give them some time to get familiar with him again. When returning him back to the center, I said to him, **"We did it! We made it happen." He was happy and proud of himself,** so was I. Even more so, he is still teaching me how to **love unconditional, detachment, compassion, patience, acceptance, and inner and over-standing of myself and my life purpose.** He now allows me to kiss him on his cheek without having a **panic attack**, or I will ask him to kiss me without him **resisting** and **looking crazy with fear. I realized my inner work** was truly beginning when I woke up the next day (Sunday), knowing he was there with me **(connected)** for the first time. Feeling love and inner-stand for him in my heart now, I could see him more clearly; the harmony flowed.

I was experiencing the feeling of being in heaven with him. I thanked the God within for these revelations and the opportunity to learn how to reconnect to what was always there from the beginning. Admitting the truth can be difficult because it requires us to really look at ourselves, examining and exposing our true feelings, motives, faults and actions.   I really, really feel my father when I don't see him now!   I truly feel my father has always been a good example or an excellent warning. Either way, it worked for me. I got the Divine Lessons his life lessons offered me- Like one of Dr. Martin L. King post card I brought said **"FREEDOM IS WORTH DYING FOR.""**

The TRUTH will set your MIND, HEART and SOUL FREE and YOUR LIFE WILL SHOW IT. -Rose W.W.

DON"T WORRY BE JOYOUS!!!

Chapter 17
Chronicles of My Life's Revelations

INFECTION & ALLERGY

I was hospitalized at the age of twenty-three, at Bronx Lebanon Hospital on the Grand Concourse in the Bronx. Still in an unhealthy marriage with three children, I was experiencing severe pain on the top back of the right side of my head and a very high fever. That was the first and only time I had a spinal tap done. The intern doctor injected me about six or eight times trying to get some fluid; he said my spine was like that of a ninety-year-old woman's, it was painful and any **movement could have paralyzed me. My roommate** who was a mature lady in the medical field, told the intern to stop and go get a **real doctor** because he really didn't know what he was doing. Another doctor came and did the **spinal tap 1-2-3** and a bone marrow extraction, seeing a **needle that thick going in my right hip bone was extremely petrifying.**

There was severe pain and I was bedridden for twenty-four hours following the procedures. They took many different tests thinking it could be some type of brain infection, but nothing was ever confirmed.

After being there about five days, the fever broke on its own accord and the pain subsided. I was then released and sent home. Looking back, I now inner and over-stand the fever burnt out **the toxic bacteria** that was caused by my **negative mental attitude** at that time in my life. However, **the real cause was my state of mind being in an unhappy abusive marriage, feeling unloved, fearful. And powerless, these are all** states of **VICTIM CONSCIOUSNESS and UNHEALTHY DIET.**

I was treated many times at **Bronx Lebanon** on **Fulton Avenue** in the Bronx N. Y. for severe skin allergies. **My skin would itch intensely and I would break out with hives, bumps, lumps, and swelling all over my**

body and **mainly my face so badly that I looked like** I was in a fight **with Joe Fraser.** The allergies were so severe I had to get injections to open up my breathing passages. The doctors performed every allergy test, and every result was negative. **Once I finally tapped into the courage I didn't realize I had deep inside of me, finally leaving my unhappy and abusive marriage years later, those symptoms never occurred again to that degree.**

TRANSFORMATION

God has proved her/his truths to me. **In the early 1990's,** I was still partying in clubs in Manhattan about three times a week. **I remained open minded, learning how to listen to the true voice from within myself reading, studying, meditating, and contemplating every new awareness that was being revealed for my spiritual growth.**

I went out this Saturday night to a club, boy! Having a great time, I danced until the club closed. Returning to my apartment about six o'clock Sunday morning, **I went fast asleep and then woke up about 9:00 am, Feeling this sudden urge to go to a church. I was totally shocked by the idea and tried to convince myself that I was too tired and sleepy,** which wasn't true because **I felt vigorous and peaceful.** So, I came up with another excuse why not to go...

It was raining a lot, like some say it's raining cats and dogs outside, I tried to go back to sleep but couldn't. **The thought was stirring up inside of me, it wouldn't leave me alone. I tossed and turned finally getting up to take a shower,** dressed and **went to the church on the corner of my block.**

I went to a church because I listened and trusted the urge from within to do something I really didn't want to nor had no plan to do, in the past I attended the church sometimes only because of my earlier surrounding for escapism, but this day I was being guided there to see

and participate in the religious process in order for me to witness the real hypocrisy that is a part of the religious teaching in most churches. Most of the time people go to church to escape from their unfulfilling, unhappy lives to get approval, validation, and acceptance from their leaders, congregation, and family. They wear their religion as a badge of superiority. Anyone who did not believe what they believed was the so-called Devil and was going to Hell. I can tell you about Hell and I didn't die to be there. I have experienced it many times because it's only a state of mind.

Now I am here sitting in this church very alert, listening with not just my ears, but with my heart and soul. From reading the book "Key to Your Self," I was observing everything now with new open eyes, ears, spirit and heart. When the Pastor asked if anyone wanted to give their life to God (hmm?), I tried to resist this sudden surge of energy that came up and consumed my whole being with love and peace. It' a state of just BEING.

This was not an external experience or a per-programmed or an auto pilot reaction for me.

Trying very hard to resist, I was trying to hold on to the bench to prevent me from going up to the altar. I was lifted up out of my seat and lead down the aisle by the true Spirit. Everyone was looking and smiling at me, nodding their heads approvingly because I was becoming a part of their false Matrix (Misery Loves Company and they said ignorance is BLISS). The Pastor took my hands and began saying what they say (you know what I mean), and that's when I became a member (a robot in flesh) of a church again.

I was feeling that something powerful was happening, I was being prepared for change a real wake up experience. I was being lead to my true spiritual path, not knowing where it would lead me, by committing myself to the true Creator, paying attention and not getting attached to any of the dogma of the church religion. I found out that it was not about God, just about seduction, manipulation deception for mind control, the building, and man's religion. I went through that religious process in that church for about four years. God led me in and out of the church and religion; this transformed me. The transformation, transfiguration, and transmutation were great after truly being aware of the seductiveness, deception, misinterpretation and misleading non-truths.

Most of the time we need to get lost, to find our way, to realize the right path. This experience allowed me to go deeper inside of my True self to realize God's truth in order to be an effective, powerful, sensitive, and non-egotistical a true spiritual teacher. Not to be used by the dark entities playing on both side. FRONTING as the good ones, all I had to do is go inside of myself and say YES.

FRANK

In 1987 was the beginning of my journey towards my resurrection into God consciousness. I was dealing with the dis-ease Sarcoidosis, and I also began treatment and was struggling with the transition of my dear beloved, Frank Jr. Although we were estranged mates, we maintained a good, strong, loving friendship. I was secure in my heart and mind that he would always be there for me no matter what, never thought he would die/transition (more about relationships in another book to come).His death was a reality check, and I was devastated. Strangely enough, I had a detailed premonition of Frank's transition which I wasn't aware or understood its symbolic meaning at the time. I didn't believe I was seeing a future event, until it happened. I shared this vision with Frank, he told me to stop worrying about trying to figure out who it was that I saw in my vision. At that time I did not know it was about him leaving this dimension, "what we call death" in this vision, I saw my father lying on the kitchen floor in this strange apartment; he was bleeding from his head, but what was even weirder my father had on this curly wig. In reality my father was almost bald. It just felt like he didn't belong there in that apartment.

I didn't discuss it with anyone else, because most people who are taught in religion would have said it's the work of the so-called Devil, witchcraft or voodoo. Even though they believe people in the bible had visions too they only knew what the slave master implanted in their consciousness; this turned them against true spirituality from the cosmos. I had no spiritual awareness either at that time, not realizing the vision was preparing me for Frank's death.

Frank had the Jehri curl hairstyle...hey, this was in the 80's and the apartment in the vision was unfamiliar because he was living with this young lady and her young children. He never told me he wasn't living with his sister anymore, whose apartment I was familiar with.

One Saturday night, he came over and wanted to go to a club to celebrate his new job of seven months. He was happy that an employer had finally shown their appreciation of his services with an extra-large bonus check. I didn't feel good that night. I was being treated for a Hiatus Hernia, I had eaten something greasy that day, so instead we just talked and watched the movie, "Car Wash" on the late show on television at about 2:00 Am., he left. He called me Sunday to tell me he had stopped by a club for a little while after he left my apartment, and when he woke up that morning, he had pain in his head, a sore throat. He came over that evening and said he had gargled with some peroxide and that his throat felt better. He had taken some aspirin for his headache earlier. He asked me for a few of my Motrin 800mg pain pills, which only numbed the pain. I expressed to him that he still should see a good doctor. The body pain was letting him know something was (imbalance) wrong.

79

On Monday he called me, but still haven't hadn't seen a doctor; he was still gargling and taking the pain pills. He said he was fine, "I still **insisted** go see a doctor" Tuesday **Frank still hadn't seen a doctor,** on **Wednesday night;** he called from work and asked if he could come visit me. For some reason I was **uncomfortable about him coming over that night,** I told him lovingly, "No, I'll see you tomorrow night."

I went to bed and slept until about 4:00 am. Thursday morning, **May 21, 1987,** I woke up and felt a good surge of loving energy passing over me saying good-bye; afterward, **I felt sad and perplexed.** I jumped up from the couch and said to myself, **someone I care about just made their transition (died). My first thought was my new present companion,** because his job involved traveling a lot for the **government by airplane. I didn't know who to call, so I simply prayed that this soul, whoever** it was, be in peace. I eventually fell back to sleep and woke up about 8:00 Am., feeling anxiety. **It was a warm, sunny, beautiful spring day,** about 2:00 pm. my telephone rang. It **was Frank's sister, Helen;** the one he was living with. When I picked up the phone Suddenly, I felt a **painful sinking feeling** in my **solar plexus center (gut);** I knew something was wrong and the tone in her voice verified it. She told me her brother died in his sleep that night. I couldn't speak; I told her I'd call her back. **Silence just came over me; the image of my vision was now becoming clearer.**

When I returned her call, I asked her what happened and **where did he die.** She got quiet and then said they didn't know how or why he died, avoiding the other question. She then lied and said, **"He died at my apartment."** I responded, **"If my vision was correct, he didn't die in your apartment."**

She was trying to spare me more pain. I don't really think she knew that we were both seeing other people. Truth is he died in a young lady's apartment he was living with. **Helen** said one of her young sons

80

tried to wake him up and couldn't. **I told her the vision about the bleeding from the head and the time I felt his Spirit leaving this physical plane to another level of vibration into the invisible realm.** Everything was confirmed later when the young lady he was seeing called me saying that he loved her too.

I said, "Yes, he did because if he didn't he **wouldn't have been with you." I was not trying to hurt or make her feel worse.** I can only imagine what she was truly feeling; the energy of her pain came through the phone line **she knew he wanted to be back with me.**

He had a brain aneurysm; the blood leaked from the brain flooded his heart, which caused a heart attack too. I went to his hometown in South Carolina for the funeral **(home coming). His lady friend was there too, she kept her distance from me never saying a word. The whole experience was very emotional painful Consciousness especially for his parents.** They had a very sickly daughter and never expected Frank to (transition) die first, especially since he didn't have any known **health issues.** I was sitting behind his sisters in the church when all of a sudden, **I felt this invisible presence like loving arms embracing me and I knew was alright. The emotional pain subsided** and I use the experience to teach and empower myself. **Then I was able to console one of his sisters.** I didn't want to see them put his body in the ground; **I looked at him when they were bringing him into the church. I brought one rose which I left with him. I don't believe in spending a lot of money after the person has made their transition, I feel it's all too commercialized for profits and they play on our emotions pain or quilt.**

When I returned to NYC, I went into a numb state for about three months I just slept most of the time. My best friend Dorothy called every night for a while to help me through the grieving healing process.

I never thought that at thirty-five he would be gone, **I was selfish I made his death unconsciously about me,** who was going to be there for me that I could count on, if my new relationships don't work out. Years later I realized I saw frank as my safety net, that's why I took his transition like I did. Thankfully I have (learned) evolved since then as a result of the Creator showing me that the way out was actually by going deeper within myself. Frank is still with me in my heart. He comes to me in dreams or visions; he gives me wisdom and insight to help me **reach higher levels of God consciousness.** He had a zest for this physical life. **Thank you, Frank; stay in my heart.**

CAR-ACCIDENT

In August 1966, on a nice warm evening, **my companion at that time** was my first child's father. We had an **argument** and I left his sister's apartment very upset. **I was hit by a car on Intervale Avenue** near **Westchester Avenue in the** Bronx, N. Y. **I don't remember if I deliberately jumped in front of that car or if I was upset and didn't see the car. It really didn't matter because I attracted the car to hit me, consciously or unconsciously, because of my state of mind at the time.** I was told I was knocked upwards and onto the other side of **Intervale Avenue**, which is a very wide street. The point I am making is the **reason a very specific part of my body was injured**...my head. I was **knocked unconscious,** had a large bruise on the right side of my head, due to my **unconscious state of mind holding anger, tension, confusion, and all kinds of fear from my parents unconscious life style which is why certain parts of my body were affected. I also suffered a fractured pelvis bone with severe pain; this injury left me with a limp for months. The emotions related to this injury were me being afraid to move forward in my life and feeling like a victim.** I unconsciously harbored **feelings** inside, such as **shame, hurt, anger and hatred for my parents, fear of my future and moving forward (related to the leg injury)** which was directly related to the **symptoms of my emotions**). My fears and

82

holding onto negative thoughts about myself and beliefs had to do with my confusion at that time **(related to the head injury).**

I was taken and treated at the old Lincoln Hospital in the Bronx; however, no x-rays were taken and I was released. A few days later due to the **head injury and severe pain in my pelvis area,** I was told a neighbor observed me and said that something was wrong and I was taken to another city hospital **that did x-rays this time.** They discovered I had a **fractured pelvis. (HMM, LAW SUIT)**

My total healing process took nine months; the doctors thought I would have a limp or wouldn't be able to have any more children without complication. **A couple of years later, I had my daughter, and years later delivered my youngest son with no difficulty.**

FOOT-OPERATION

The beginning of **October 2004,** I went to the foot clinic in Manhattan, where I was examined for two very painful hammer toes on my right foot. **The doctors and interns were very kind and efficient at their jobs. They said I needed foot surgery; the bones on two toes were bent upward and rubbing against any shoes I would wear. They scheduled me for surgery at Metropolitan Hospital on October 22nd. During the first week** I took all the necessary tests including my blood pressure test, which was better than normal because I **had just finished meditating before they took it.** When the **urine, blood and cholesterol test results** returned, all three were the same - **superb!**

I asked the doctor **what caused the callus; he said it was the way the body way of protecting the bone pushing up and rubbing against my shoe. Then, the doctor asked me about my family medical history.** I responded, "**Healthy!**"

He looked at me like I had two heads, asking if there was any **diabetes, hypertension, cancer,** and so on and so on. This time I looked at him like he had **two heads.** I meant what I said "Health runs in my family," I believe **most diseases** are **learned behavior and thought patterns pasted down in most cases from generation.** I wasn't going to allow them to **perpetuate** that mindset in my **subconscious mind** again. I have no intention of creating anything I don't want because energy follows thoughts. And I am listening to my higher-self. **One of the intern doctor started calling me the holistic patient. We had a good conversation (he thought I was very interesting to talk to), and he asked me about my beliefs and why I believed them. I told him I believed because of my good test results (evident). I recommended the book** "The Power of Your Subconscious Mind" by Dr. Joseph Murphy.

My brother, Corrie Jr., escorted me to the **hospital,** before the surgery, the doctor had me **sign a disclaimer.** I asked **what's the side effects of the surgery would be,** to which he replied **my toes could turn black and blue, stay numb, or fall off. I wasn't worried because Spirit had already assured me that everything was good.** After the procedure, I woke up from the anesthesia feeling a little pressure in my head. The doctor gave me a **prescription for pain pills (NUMB) with codeine for my foot. Hey! They cut some bone off of my toes; that doesn't tickle! Before leaving the hospital, the doctor showed me how to use the cane to help me balance and walk. When my brother and I returned to my apartment, he asked if I was going to be alright, after assuring him I would be, he said he would return later.**

About twenty minutes later, the **anesthesia completely wore off;** my head and foot were in excruciating pain. I couldn't even **think straight,** and I **forgot to let my brother get the prescription filled.** I tried calling **my dear friend Tracy** from around the corner and her **daughter Jamila,** because they live the closest to me, after the third try I was ready to

84

crawl to my front door and **holler for anyone to help me**. I didn't care who! I finally managed to get her telephone number correct, and they came right away. As they walked in they looked **afraid and confused** at how I looked they were so used to me being the strong one. **(I am learning not to be afraid to ask the right person for help)**. They had never seen me in pain, I asked Tracy to give me a wet hot cloth for my head, and she said **"You mean a cold cloth, right?"** I responded, "No, **my Spirit said hot."** Within five minutes of applying it to the right side of my head, the pain was gone. **Tracy got the prescription filled**, after taking one pain pill; I experienced a floating sensation and saw beautiful colors. **I felt free flowing, oneness and blissful, just like** when I meditate and reach that level of **ecstasy naturally and very mystical.** However, this was a **negative chemical induced feeling, but it felt good!**

That was such a **great, wonderful, joyous weekend, with lots of laughter. Many of my friends and two of my family members stayed close by to assist me in every way,** they didn't even want me to go to the bathroom alone. They were trying to help me walk with the cane; I walked better without it or their help! **Don't get me wrong I was very grateful to the Creator for providing great people in my life that showed me love and cared for me at that moment.** We had a wonderful weekend watching DVD s, and eating. **I even made jokes in spite of my pain everyone was laughing and having a great time. I chose not to play the victim role and healed quicker as a result.**

"Every word of God is pure; he/she is a shield unto them that truly put their trust in thee." -Proverbs 30:5

VOMITING
January 31, 2005, Friday evening, **I was feeling just great!** I was sitting at the sewing machine while on the phone with my best friend Bernice

and all of a sudden I began to **feel nauseous and sick.** I ate healthy and consumed nothing out of the ordinary that day, but I began to vomit on and off around 4:30 pm. I couldn't stop. **My youngest son Cliff** came home about 9:30 pm. He realized something was **seriously wrong** with me. He pleaded with me to let him take me to the doctor I said **"No, I'll be fine."** I had **never vomited** like that in my life! Becoming a little afraid I said **"God, I don't want to die tonight."** Just then a feeling engulfed me saying, **"You will be just fine."** I asked **Cliff** to make me some **herbal tea,** and after drinking it I threw it back up, he then gave me some **aloeceutical herbal stomach formula, my body was rejecting everything. Then all of a sudden the muscles in my whole upper body and torso got tight as a knot and I was in excruciating pain. My Spirit said, "Lay down."** I asked my son for a heating pad. He massaged my neck, shoulders, and felt how tight my muscles were down to my fingertips. I went to my bed placed a pail beside it because I was still vomiting. I tried to stay relaxed by doing deep breathing from my diaphragm. My son slept on the couch to be near me, just in case I needed him to rush me to the hospital, and finally I fell asleep. Saturday morning, I woke up feeling great, reborn, and renewed. I was inspired to rest all day, eat light, drink plenty of liquids mainly water, and that's exactly what I did. The body knows what it needs, if we just learn how to listen, trust and obey.

Sunday that was the day of the **Self-Awareness free seminar** a **free seminar** I gave a every last Sunday of the month, on this particular Sunday I was more than ready for it. **We had a full room with mostly new people and they were great too!** They seemed to be **open and receptive** to what I was being expressed, I couldn't even tell you what I said that day because every word just flowed through me like never before. **Everyone showed me love and thanked me.** Even my daughter said to me that I was at my very best, and that she was on the edge of her seat; she and others said I was glowing! She said that this seminar was even better than the fabulous first one I gave for the gay community in 2003. She jokily says that I should vomit prior to all of my seminars. My true spirit revealed to me that my body detoxified itself. If I had gone to a doctor they would have given me something to stop the vomiting; it would have interrupted the natural purification process. Believe me when I say whatever was in me that needed to be released was expelled. Faith and trust in the true Spirit within that source will you get you through anything. **Ignorance kills most people.**

HIP

In March of 2005, I experienced severe pain in my left hip. Sleeping was difficult, if I moved a certain way, it would cause more pain. When **I began walking with a little limp,**   I decided to go to Montefiore Hospital's emergency room. The technicians took x-rays of my hip and didn't find anything wrong. **I was then referred to the department of Orthopedic Surgery; I was examined there on April 6, 2005 by a young Caucasian male doctor who insisted they needed to do their own set of x-rays. I disagreed and informed him that I just took x-rays a week ago; it was all part of the same medical center. I over-stood; it's all about the money!**

I consented to taking the second set of x-rays, and of course he did not find anything different. He didn't realize until he focuses on my chart that I was fifty-four; he thought I was thirty-five. Once he realized my age, he said it could be **arthritis starting to set** in and eventually, I would probably have to get a **hip replacement.(age had nothing to do with it, don't believe the HYPE!)** He continued to say that he was in his thirties and was experiencing some arthritis pain too, as if to make his diagnosis valid for me. I looked at him like **he was crazy,** and in my mind **dismissed him, didn't give what he was saying any power,** I am not him. **Why do we choose to believe everything doctors say or**

87

anyone, without real facts, in most cases, without thinking, questioning or researching and meditating?) He wrote a prescription for me that I never filled), he told me not to worry it wasn't **viOXX** (that was taken off the market at that time, because of causing some death and other health problems). Then his assistant took me in a room and to my surprise, told me to drop my pants to give an injection for the pain. When I declined he became annoyed, saying, "If you want to stay in pain, it's alright with me." **I didn't take it personal.**

First, the doctors really didn't know what was causing the pain; secondly, **I didn't know what was in the needle.** Therefore my body and spirit told me not to take it. That week I listened to my body, spirit, and I bought some Tiger Balm ointment, rubbed it on the area every night, and applied a heating pad. **I did deep breathing for ten minutes, focused on a white, gold or blue healing light from my mind's eye (the third eye), said a prayer of thanks and meditated, affirming and feeling the healing.** I called on the healing energy within my **awakening Christ consciousness.**

Mother's Day (which is everyday), I asked my three children not to buy me **flowers, jewelry, or give me a card with money. I simply wanted them to take me to Roseland' Oldies but Goodies dance night** and just have fun with me, just being together **enjoying the moment;** I danced to just about every song (hey**!) I even went down to the floor many times with no problem getting up.** My children looked at me amazed, and **Shine** the youngest said to me with delight in his eyes, a **big smile,** and a hug, **"You are a party animal,"** which he meant in a good fun way. (You know what I mean). I wish that doctor was there to see me, there will never be a **hip replacement** for me, that pain was transformed. Whatever was **out of balance, I aligned my energy and worked through it, having a shift in consciousness, and gave thanks to the universe for all of my healing lessons and blessings.**

"Whatever ye shall ask in (true) prayer, believe you shall receive. -Matthew 21:22

GOD CAN SPEAK THROUGH ANYONE Friday morning, September 16, 2005, I woke up feeling really great reflecting on my life. We had just celebrated my 55th birthday and anniversary party on September 10th with my three children, my brother Mickey, my sister Edna, and even my father, my God-daughter Mist, and her wonderful mother and brother, who came up from Virginia just for my party, and mostly all true friends; even the ones who couldn't attend were there in spirit. I also for the first time met some people who were viewers and supporters of my cable show; I was so grateful to meet them. Earlier that evening I celebrated with the children in my neighborhood; I am truly loved and blessed by the right people. What others think of me is none of my business. Later that morning, my brother came over with the DVD Instinct, with Anthony Hopkins and Cuba Gooding Jr. It's about an anthropologist, who becomes a primate to find the lost realities of our natural instincts and must be reverted back to the reality of the so-called human idealism by the psychiatrist, I know that since then I have grown spiritually to a higher consciousness. I watched certain parts of the movie; I cried and shouted out in pain for all of God's children. I said, how did we allow ourselves to stay on such low vibration in consciousness, suffering so long and being controlled? Everyone's acting was superb especially Gooding Jr. and Hopkins. If any movie deserves great recognition, it's this one. It's one of the best to me for all the right reasons: positive, inspiring truthful loving, and thought invoking to me, the best part of the movie was when Mr. Hopkins was choking Mr. Gooding; he made him write down, "what have taken from you," which was the (illusion). And that we are TAKER. WE don't really care about others; long as we get what we are programmed to want (Checkt- Jim Keady vs. Nike and St. John University). Everyone doesn't sell out for money and fame.

I started feeling like a failure like I really wasn't affecting some greater change in people's mindset. **I want to help people come out of the illusion of only the physical and material world.** I said to the God "This was in 2005 and I have been teaching for **over ten years** now, there are so many people still lost. Maybe this is bigger than me." **I felt discouraged and was ready to give up.** Suddenly my phone rang **Mr. Carter** who is a faithful viewer of my show and loves the messages my quests and I share, **he highly praised** me on how I have **inspired, motivated, encouraged, empowered and enlightened him.** He also thanked the Creator for me being a beacon of light in his life, and I know he is a light in my life.

He praised me even more than he did when he first called me **on April 16, 2005. Thank you, Mr. Carter** for your genuine love, praise, inspiration, and for giving me the courage to continue my SOUL purpose for being here on this continuous, challenging journey being a vessel for the **PRIME CREATOR** to work through.

The next day, I went to the **Bronx Zoo** with myself and **really enjoyed nature's animals, especially the gorillas they have a lot to teach us. You must see the movie Instinct again and again!**

Write what you felt was profound about the movie and why, once you view it, and you can send me an e-mail.

"If any of you lack wisdom, let him ask of God that give to all men liberally, and upbraideth not, and it shall be given him."   -James 1:5

Chapter18
Two Different Reality

My Godmother, Magnolia, believed in two powers, God and the (so-called) Devil. Her vision was obscured; it appeared to her that some people and situations were good while others were **bad or evil**. She gave the **(so-called) Devil** more **credibility**, not understanding that there is really only one presence and power - **THE FORCE, God (Yahweh, Eloheem called by many names),** which is good as everything is of God it's **how we perceive experiences.** She never went through the **spiritual crucifixion of the false self-due to false beliefs,** to learn from and **embrace our dark side.** Whatever her religion had been teaching her was **stagnating to her spiritual growth for awakening to Christ** consciousness, there was no raising her consciousness for evolution back to GODHEAD.

She needed a true resurrection to realize the realm of Infinite Eternal Being, the Kingdom of Heaven, and our true home within ourselves. She needed to realize that God is everywhere when we fully examine a so-called bad experience transcend and transform and inner and over-stand the lessons needed for spiritual growth, to get us back to true reality. (God Consciousness the Kingdom of Heaven can only be reached through a higher state of vibration frequency.

My strongest inspiration to finish this book was when **Divine Spirit** channeled through my beloved Godmother Magnolia, while she was getting ready to make her transition because I never wrote a book and was afraid, who will want to read it how people would judge me. I was ready to GIVE-UP many times; I heard that small voice saying DON"T.

June 5, 2002, about 4:00 Am., on a warm peaceful morning, I was awakened by a strong, loving burst of energy penetrating my whole being, every cell, atom, and molecule. I felt a sense of clarity, freedom, harmony, and a deep sense of purpose with this overwhelming urge to just write. It was like the pen had a mind of its own. I couldn't stop writing for hours, even if I wanted to I felt the energy saying, "Tell the truth, and tell your story and mine." I didn't understand what was happening. I just allowed the energy to flow through myself to the pen to the paper, and then I realized what was being written was part of my story which involved our experience together and how our life together unfolded, that I didn't plan to write about not knowing she was hospitalized at that particular time.

Later that morning about 8:00 Am., while I was still writing, my phone rang. It was Magnolia's other goddaughter (I'll call her Ann) called from her job to say she had been trying to reach her by phone but no one answered. I replied that I would try calling her. I didn't get a response either; I called Barbara back and told her I'd try calling some hospitals to see if she had been admitted.

The previous morning (on June 4th), Ann called me saying she had called her and that our **Godmother's** sister had answered the **phone informing her that our godmother wasn't feeling well and didn't feel like talking.** Ann asked me to call her knowing that she would talk to me yes I did. When I called her sister picked up the phone and told her it was me, she did speak with me! She told me that her body just didn't feel right. I asked her if she wanted me to come and take her to the doctor, to which she replied, "No, I'll be alright." The day before her sister had taken her to **Montefiore Hospital** the waiting was too long for her so she left without seeing a doctor; I knew how impatient she could be especially with herself. That same day I was scheduled to be interview about my spirituality on **The Gilchrist Experience cable show in Manhattan N.Y.** My godmother didn't want me to cancel, saying, "**People need to hear what you have to say; it will truly help** change their lives." I made her promise me that she'd go back and see a doctor if she felt worse, she's an Aries and can be very stubborn at times. While visiting her I had tried to talk her into letting me take her to the doctor the morning before **June 3rd.** We spent most of that day **(June 3rd)** talking and bonding (Really) I just listened to her speaking from her living room recliner chair. She became very quiet looking really sad, fearful, hurt, confused, and disappointed. Then she looked at me with the sad eyes of a child, tears rolling down her cheeks, and said, "Do you think God is punishing me?"

I was torn up inside, feeling her emotional pain, which was far worse than all the physical pain she had endured most of all her life. I tried again to help her deprogram her mind of false concepts about God, explaining that God (Spirit) doesn't punish or condemn us, that we punish ourselves by on false concept of who and what GOD is and our misuse of Universal Laws and misinterpretation of life's principles and not TRUSTING, VALUE and KNOWING our TRUE DIVINE BEAUTIFUL SELF.

Magnolia had many health conditions, she shared with me some of her **painful childhood experiences going back many years,** expressing about being sick as an infant with a nervous condition and having very high fevers. As an adult, she had high blood pressure, a thyroid problem, arthritis, allergies, poor circulation, and problems with her liver and eyes. God only knew what else was wrong with here!

Facing and Feeling the pain starts the healing process and opening the heart center.

BE TRUE TO WHOM YOU TRULY ARE, (SOUL) KNOW SELF!

People punish themselves unconsciously by engaging in self-destructive thinking, feeling unconsciously unhappy etc., CREATING Arthritis, Lung and Thyroid problem, High blood pressure, Cancer, Diabetes, Joint pain, Hysterectomy, Obesity, etc., attracting some kind of Accident to themselves and the list continue.

I heard someone say that ignorance kills, but I like it written this way better:

Ignorance doesn't kill; it's what you know that's not true! -RW

LEARNING TO REMEMBER!

Chapter 19
Releasing

One year before my godmother's transition, I felt she was unconsciously preparing to leave the physical dimension. Her fears grew more profound; it was in her eyes and face and I heard it in her voice. She shared more and more about her unhappy childhood and some of what she really felt about certain family members and her church family in New York.

One day in the spring of 2001, she phoned me asking what other herbs she could take "because her body just didn't feel right." She knew I had taken a beginner's course in **herbology**; she had been drinking herb teas and taking herbal extracts since I met her **in 1978. I insisted she let me take her to a doctor; we went to Montefiore's Outpatient Department** that morning to see her doctors who have been treating her for years. **While sitting in that waiting room for hours she started telling me some things about her childhood that was very painful for her.** Things such as when her mother had taken her out of school (she was the fourth child) so that she could help take care of the younger children, especially the twin babies. She said, **"Back then there were no Pampers." (Hmm)**

She really resented having her **education interrupted.** She continued saying with lots of emotion that since she **had to help care for her younger siblings, she never wanted children of her own. When she became an adult and married,** she became pregnant and had a miscarriage, and had to have a **hysterectomy, a self-fulfilling prophecy.**

She was still **holding resentment toward her mother, herself, and feeling guilty** for it because of the **false religious beliefs she held.** "Honor thy mother and thy father," the **mis- concept is what she was** taught to believe; however her feelings of **resentment** toward her mother could not co-exist with her **fear and misconception** about her religious beliefs. **Having feelings of guilt bring punishment (self-inflicted pain).**

Judgment - The description of the last judgment, as given in the gospel, has been used to terrify men and women, and thus, compel them to unite with the church; but in this day of enlightenment, people are not so easily led or driven by fear. They ask for understanding. When they seek light concerning the judgment, it is given, and they learn that the judgment is all a matter of divine law. They find that for every departure from this law they must suffer, not in some future time or greater tribulation, not in a great judgment after death, but in this life here and now.

Metaphysical Bible Dictionary by Unity (page 376)

Every thought clothes itself in a life form according to the characteristics given it by the thinker (self-fulfilling prophecy). Magnolia never learned how to express embrace those negative emotions to heal, **forgive herself and others and to surrender,** more than anything she **wanted to be the perfect daughter for her mother** (which I can relate to...the subject of another book I am writing). **She believed she needed her mother's approval, acceptance to be loved. She followed and accepted her mother's religious doctrine without ever questioning or researching it, without allowing herself to have her own experience for her own unique self-discovery.** She shared with me some things her sisters had done as teenagers that her mother didn't approve of. I feel that **making mistakes is part of life's lessons and challenges** for the individual to learn, grow and to re-discover their true self to evolve. Her sisters **were choosing their own experiences and make their mistakes** (sound like they had some fun to). **I felt she had missed out on some of the adolescent and teen fun and adventures experiences** to learn for

96

you, not to get **stuck in fear and conformity** like most **parents just existing! Following** someone else's **FALSE CONSTRUCT.**

Next, she began talking about her **parents' marriage** which she felt wasn't good, her mother had **settled** and **stayed in an unhappy, unhealthy, no personal growth and unfulfilled marriage** and her mother had lots of health issues, too! **I was happy** when the doctor called her into the examining room because the more **she reflected on her childhood,** the more I saw and felt her anger, and **underneath anger is hurt**...lots of hurt. **The doctor took some tests,** prescribed her more pills for the **thyroid,** and scheduled her to come back in six weeks. **I didn't feel good about her examination.**

A few weeks later, she called this time her **right foot and ankle were swollen and had broken out in a rash!** I insisted on taking her to see a different doctor or taking her to the **emergency room at Montefiore** Hospital, she had a strong dislike for emergency rooms and had not been to one (that I know of) in at least sixty years not likening the all-day wait to be seen. **I convinced her to let me take her.** After a few hours of waiting and me still listening to her about her life, **I knew she was trying to release years and years of suppressed difficult painful feelings and didn't want to feel quilt or judged on how she really felt all her life I listen.** They called her and examined her foot and put her on a stretcher for about two more hours. **She became upset, wanted to leave, feeling she was taking up my whole day. I told her, "We're staying as long as it takes because if it was me, you would stay with me all day and night."**

After hours of waiting they finally took some blood tests and x-rays. While waiting, she continued talking to me then asked, **"Am I talking too much?"** "No!" I exclaimed. Her favorite saying was that **the Devil is trying to destroy her mind or body.** She stopped talking for a while and during the break, while I was reading my book **Songs of God by Joseph Murphy**, I showed her **a different interpretation of scripture that made sense, which empowered the self and expanded the mind. I** had given her the book a few months ago and soon after that she asked me for five more copies to send to people close to her heart, people she thought were more open minded than her, meanwhile here she was reading some little religious pamphlet that was perpetuating the same old negative nonsense powerless,

SELF –VICTIMLIZATION that helped got her in the condition and had her waiting for someone other than her **HIGHERSELF** to come back and save her from herself.

James 5:13-18 the prayer of faith will save the one who is sick.

Religion and the role of most authority figures, such as the Reverend, Pastor, Bishop, Pope, etc. are all designed to **revert us back to our obedient childhood state of mind,** seeking praises, approval and love we feel we didn't get from our parents. Most of those leaders are really entertainers. My godmother felt like she couldn't liberate her mind from **coercion and seduction** because of her programming, going to church every week, **listening to most gospel music and sermons at home only re-enforced the programming.**

It was all being subliminally reinforced with a little of the truth and some good sounding music that kept her in that **hypnotic victim state** of mind (the illusion), **denying her underlying social emotional, and spiritual needs. I freed myself by reclaiming them.**

Mind washing - The process of systematically, powerfully, and profoundly indoctrinating a person to weaken or destroy their ideas and beliefs. You become willing to accept their (whoever) beliefs and ideas. A belief without facts and common sense is stupidity.
-Rose Whaley

Crucifixion - The crossing out in consciousness of errors that have become fixed states of mind; the surrender or death of the whole personality in order that the Christ Mind Releasing may be expressed in all its fullness. The crucifixion of Jesus represents the wiping of personality out of consciousness. We deny the human self so that we may unite with the selfless. We give up the mortal so that we may attain the immortal. We dissolve the thought of the physical body so that we may realize the spiritual body. - Charles Fillmore (page 46)

After the doctors finished all my godmother's tests and told her the results, gave her medication and scheduled a follow-up appointment, we left. While we were leaving she said, "The doctor said I have a liver condition, which I was told over twenty years ago." I was outraged that she had kept that to herself and not gotten any treatment, I said, "Why didn't you get some help? Why would you do this to yourself?"

With sad eyes she didn't say a word, here I was looking at this 81-year-old lady, whom I loved dearly, and seeing her wounded inner child that never, never learned how to heal. She had been running away, covering up, and suppressing her true unconscious feelings all her life, trying to get to the light by avoiding darkness, which is a part of ourselves we don't want to face and acknowledge. Darkness represents all our false fears, envy, competitiveness false ego and deficiencies, not confronting these feelings and carrying the shame, guilt, anger, and disappointments. By learning how to forgive, heal, and truly love ourselves and others, we can heal by facing and working through the pain. Taking back our natural power that God has given us within! We need reconnect to our Soul SELF. A flashlight with no battery is dead; it has no power.

When everything was finished at the emergency room, we took a cab to her apartment and I made sure she was conformable. When I returned to my apartment I could not stop thinking about her and feeling her pain. I cried for her wounded inner child that was desperately trying to come through the darkness and get into the light which represents the truth to heal and free your soul/consciousness, darkness represent ignorance of the truth. That day really taught me a lot. I was receptive to all the growth lessons. **She was just happy that I was there with her all day...and I meant all day!**

About a year before her transition, Spirit inspired me to visit her at least once a week no matter what, to give her the most valuable thing I had - my time and love. It was all she really wanted from me; she knew she had my love. It wasn't until that year I gave her more of my time, one day a week, usually a Tuesday I would arrive at her apartment about 10:00 am, and stay for about six hours just talking, listening, and bonding with her. Maybe three times that year we went to the store. When I went to her apartment I would ride the #2 or #5 train and got off at Jackson Avenue where it crosses Westchester Avenue in the Bronx. I would pass this Korean fruit and vegetable market, where I bought her a beautiful little bunch of mixed flowers every week that year. She loved having those flowers! As my visits continued **I got to the point where it was no longer of any use trying to help to deprogram her, at this point in her life she just needed someone that she felt she could trust to hear her and to validate her pent-up feelings without being judged.** Those painful emotions she had become accustomed to, she had **inadvertently turned inward on herself, which manifested into disharmony (illnesses).** This is what had destroyed her, like so many of us do **without realizing the truth.** Whenever someone **including myself** said "**anything good or gave her a gift she would ask,**" "**Why me?** What did I do to deserve this?" I didn't like when she said things like that. **She was really saying that she wasn't worthy and didn't deserve it. (You** get the picture?) I would just smile and said, "If anyone deserves good, it's you."

She tried pretending she was happy like most people and that everything was alright by going to church, which she was addicted too, trying to fill a void inside of her with the things external (something outside of her). You can't fill the void from the outside, but we all try! We really truly have to do it from within ourselves. The outside reflects what's going on in the inside.

"Behold the Kingdom of God is within you." - Luke 17:21

Heaven - Evolving to the level of Christ consciousness where the Divine mind resides; living in a state of harmony; our thoughts of God's Kingdom in every aspect of our life; is everywhere present, being joyous, healthy, pain free, prosperous; having peace of mind; feeling powerful.
-Rose Whaley

King Solomon said, "Wisdom is the principal thing! Therefore, get wisdom," (Proverbs 4:7-8).

Wisdom is the awareness of the presence, the power of Spirit (God) within us, and the capacity to align with the Infinite, to overcome all problems, difficulties, and limitations. She kept waiting for Jesus, which became her comfort zone all her life, like it does for so many people. It's really addicted escape mechanism, the constant waiting, waiting, and waiting! Life is a gift; live life to the fullest now! All you have is right now this moment, live in the moment, live in the present! When we cannot cope with and face the pain and fears of our lives (we refer to them as adversaries instead of challenges), we find ways of trying to run or cover up our false feelings of inadequacy. We live in a state of denial, lies, deception, and people become enraged and will fight to defend them. Learning to trust and depend on your Goddess/Godself is one of the difficult and greatest challenges you'll ever undergo. We can only worship this energy force we call God, Spirit to Spirit, (Philippians 2:3) in meditation (higher consciousness).

"When FALSE FEARS ARE BANISHED, ignorance is destroyed!" -Rose Whaley

Satan is the "Devil," a state of mind formed by man's personal ideas of his power and completeness and sufficiency apart from God. Besides at times puffing up the personality, this satanic thought often turns about and, after having tempted one to do evil, discourages the soul by accusing it of sin. Summed up, it is the state of mind in man that believes in its own sufficiency independent of its creative Source. Rebellion against God under hard experiences is another form of this "hater." The personality that disbelieves in God and acknowledges no law save that of man is satanic. The Greek word that is translated "devil" in Luke 4:1-13 means accuser of the critical one. Personality describes the meaning more fully than any other word in the English language. -Metaphysical Bible Dictionary by Unity (page 575) "And the seventy returned with joy, saying, 'Lord, even the demons are subject to us in your name.'" -Luke 10:17

Chapter 20
Blinded By Deception

Over the years, my godmother's body continued to **degenerate**. For example, back **in 1996**, Monday morning, she called telling me she was taken to the emergency room due to falling down after Sunday church service. I arrived at her apartment within an hour. She looked **frightened, confused, and her arm was in a slant**. She pulled up her blouse showed me **her breast** and along the side of that area, which was black/ blue, swollen and causing her a lots of pain. She said her body just didn't feel right. She said what she always said when something not good happens to her: **"The Devil is trying to destroy my body."** **Nonsense!** Again I didn't want to hear it, I was upset. A bruise like that on someone her age meant she was seriously hurt again, she told me that the **lobby floor of the church was in need of proper repair for about a year. Now whose fault was that?** I responded angrily, "Your church owns just about half the block and maybe a lot more. Certainly they can **afford a professional to repair that floor!"**

I checked on her every day as she started to heal. During that first week she told me some **church member** called and said she ought to **sue the church. I agreed!** But because of her programming and conditioning, she responded, "That's the Devil talking." "Hmm" (That was GOD talking) I told her the church is just a building and has nothing to do with **True Spirit (God) consciousness. (Readers,** please look up the word **"deception and seduction"** in several different dictionaries, and read it until its meaning sinks **deep into your or subconscious mind so you can remember the truth and who you truly are!**

Suggestion (meaning) – ideas implanted in the mind without facts. Who is shaping your beliefs? The Jehovah's Witness, Baptist, Catholics, 7 Day Adventist, Christians, Protestants, Advertisement, Politicians, pimps in the church or on the street, etc. -Rose Whaley

Sacrifices to the Lord - (Meta) a refining process that is constantly going on in consciousness. Every thought and act of man sets free an energy that gravitates to its appointed place in the various realms of mind and body. The Lord is the one universal mind, which is the receptacle of all thought. If you have a thought of love and goodwill, you set free invisible emanations that are impregnated with these ideas. These ascend to a higher realm and form part of your soul, and at the same time relate you to the Lord, who is presiding Oversoul of the race. This is the inner meaning of offering sacrifices to the Lord. Everything in nature is going through this refining process, and there is a constant ascension of matter to mind and mind to Spirit. We are taught that a period will finally come when the whole universe will be resolved back into its original essence in God. We must purify our mind and body in order that divine Spirit can do the regenerative work. Some people think it necessary to cleanse the mind only and let the body take care of itself. Truth reveals itself; we must in all ways fulfill the law of purity. Whoever defiles his body with impure thoughts, lustful passions, or decaying food will find his progress retarded. The burnt offerings of bullocks and sheep on the altar represent the transmutation of the physical forces to the next higher plane of action. This is a process of body refinement that pertains to those who follow Jesus in the regeneration. The altar represents the place in consciousness where we are willing to give up the lower to the higher, the personal to the impersonal, and the animal to the spiritual.

The life forces of those living in generation flow to the generative center in the body and are spent in materialism, this brings death to the body. When through a sincere desire for things spiritual man lifts his mind, there is a complete reversal of these life forces. Instead of a downward flow, the currents start toward the heart and a process of body rejuvenation begins. Then there is rejoicing in the man and he sings praises to the Lord. This is represented by the "singing with loud instruments unto Jehovah." (See II Chronicles 30:13-27) When this blessed realization of the regeneration comes to consciousness, the voices of men are heard by the Lord and their prayers ascend "even unto heaven." When we have faith in God and the ways of Spirit, we are willing to give up all our material pleasures, if such be the instruction of the inner guide, the Holy Spirit. This is a point that is also symbolized by the sacrifices so often referred to in the history of the Children of Israel.

-Metaphysical Bible Dictionary by Unity (page 565)

Then I replied, **"Are you telling me that the so-called Devil has more power than the God you believe in?** Which he can make you fall, but God couldn't keep you safe in the so-called House of God?" (Somebody help me here!) **She became very quiet.**

September 2001, my godmother said she had fallen again in her church after being accidentally hit when someone stretched out their arm. I thought to myself that her GOD was trying to tell her something. How hard we work at rejecting, denying, resisting, and justifying to not changing. We look for permanence in a world where nothing remains the same; look at the trees, the flowers everything begins ripens, falls, and begins again - everything including you and me! "Death" is an illusion, death is just a transition.   As I continued my weekly visits, she started giving me some of her things: jewelry, dresses, and her **favorite jacket (saying it needed some adjustment).** The main item she wanted me to have was her **beloved quilt,** which I believe was handmade by her mother, I just couldn't take it, **I wasn't ready to face the truth** that she was **unconsciously preparing to make her transition** (die) Togo to another dimension.

Denial IS A POWERFUL PSYCHOLOGICAL MECHANISM For ESCAPE, Please look up the words, and read it over and over until you inner and over-stand the meaning.

"You are the master builder of your life; the Creator gave you everything you need. Believe and know your true cosmic self!"   -Rose W.

Stop beating your divine self-down because of making mistakes which are part of the learning /remembering process. But don't stay stagnated, Ignorant and keep making mistakes, especially the same mistakes.

Chapter 21
Divine Plan

The strangest thing started happening, when I left Magnolia's apartment and returned to my own, I looked in my tote bag and found money in an envelope. I couldn't figure out where the money had come from and how it got there without my knowing. Then it happened a second time, this time I called her and asked, "Are you putting envelope of money in my bag?" She simply laughed. HA! the next time I went there I kept my eyes on her hands, and when I went to the bathroom I made sure I took my bag with me. When I was leaving her apartment I kept the bag on my shoulder as we walked to the elevator. We hugged like always, later when I was sitting relaxed on the train my Spirit told me to look in my bag. **She did it again!** How? I asked myself, I couldn't figure it out. I didn't want her to do that. I **had already borrowed money from her for a project I was working on and she had insisted** I keep it as a donation. **She believes and supported my teaching. She always said I was doing God's TRUE ministry.**

One evening while I was lying down thinking what can give her for **her 80th EARTH-day** that would be very special? The answer that came was very clear and felt so right. **Spirit inspired me to give her a surprise birthday party. I never would have thought of a party because she didn't like crowds and noise. On a conscious level she said she didn't want any special attention given to her,** I knew better because she felt unworthy. Unconsciously she needed and wanted it. Crowds and noise, she said, made her too nervous all her life she went to church the **preacher screaming, and dancing, people jumping up and running around thinking they were moved by the true Holy Spirit,** that's what happens when you are programmed to **REACT (AUTO PILOT).** **Spirit also communicated to me that she never had a birthday party, thinking of my plan to give her one elated me, even though I didn't have the money and didn't know how I was going to manifest it and I didn't know whom to invite,** because the only thing she really did was go to church. I said to Spirit, "If you want me to do this, you already have a plan. **I surrendered everything to Divine Intelligence and just followed my inner guidance. I trusted it without a doubt. I was led to call another goddaughter of hers Ann,** who had attended the same church as her for many years. I shared with her the idea of the surprise party. **She was excited and happy to help make it a reality.** She booked the church's community room, we shared the cost of renting it and she invited people of the church she knew was close to her. Her **brother (call him) Tom from Georgia and** sent money to help pay for the food, which was good and plenty. **ANN** got a church member who did catering and she was happy to be of service. **My daughter Adrienne** and I decorated the room with **Magnolia's** favorite colors white and red. Also she made beautiful bookmarks as souvenirs for the guests. **Magnolia's family from Georgia** and other states **surprised her with their presence.** It was **a wonderful party** and her other **goddaughter Delores** brought her to the event; she was really surprised and very happy. **Spirit knew what was best when it inspired me to give the party, telling me she had never had one.**

When the party was ending, she hugged and kissed me thanking me again, she said right then if it were her time to die, she was ready to go. **She was so happy and excited being shown value and appreciated**...truly being the center of attention. **(I made sure of that!)** It **was not about the church, its members, the clergy, and especially not** the pastor. (Although a few members tried to take it there, they didn't know me (hum) and **I wasn't in that religious mindset. Besides after 50 years of her dues, donations, tithing, and services, they didn't give us the space for free!** She confirmed what Spirit had revealed to me; saying she have **never had a party.** Then she surprised me by saying **she wished her pastor would let me do spiritual workshops for the congregation, I don't know what can of look was on my face,** she smiled with that funny look on her face and said, **"But he won't."** She

108

knew why -and so do you! She was so afraid of not being righteous and in the right place by whom standard.

Righteousness - simply means the right use of universal law; right thinking, feeling, and actions.   -Rose Whaley

"Beware of practicing your righteousness before men to be noticed by them; otherwise, you have no reward with your Father [Mother] who is in heaven."   -Matthew 6:1

"But when you pray, go into your inner room [consciousness] and close the door [no conscious thoughts]. Pray to your Father [Mother] who is invisible and sees in secret and will repay you."   -Matthew 6:6

I opened my first custom-made clothing boutique in the Bronx in 1978. Magnolia's son (I'll call him) Greg was the Spirit vessel used to bring her and myself together. He came to my shop and ordered two pairs of custom made pants. When he returned for a fitting, he said he give my business card to his mother, who loved having her clothing custom made. He was with his girlfriend and they both agreed that Magnolia was hard to get along with. However, when I met her I never had any problems with her. After a few months we started spending more time together our bond got stronger our Spirits connected. Over the years we shared time together, I still have all-occasion cards she has given me, all with words of inspiration and what she add herself.

When I opened my second boutique, she surprised me with a large beautiful green plant delivered by the florist, attached was a beautiful congratulatory card handwritten, with a prayer she composed from her heart like always. She never had a problem expressing her love and support for me. I am saddened she didn't get to see me produce my cable TV show, which aired for the first time in March 2004. I thought she would live to see the manifestation of the Spiritual Center I will have one day soon. I know that she sees and is proud of what I AM DOING NOW and I still have her support, love, and blessings.

On so call Mother's Day 2002, a month before **Magnolia returned home (her transition)**, I held a fashion show and surprised her again, honoring her with a beautiful plaque, for her beautiful SPIRIT that I saw through with all her physical negative influence, but mainly her love **which she chose to share with me unconditional.** When she got up to receive the plaque and delivered a powerful speech, one I think no one who was there will ever forget. **I cherish those words in my heart, and** I am so grateful I have the videotape; I can view her saying those words again and again. A few days later, I helped her pack for a vacation. **She was going to her hometown in Georgia** and said it would be her last time **(I knew what she meant).** We spent most of the time talking. I could still see the fear in her face, eyes, voice, and I felt her **pain and disappointment** with her life it in her **aura field.**

Aura - A field of thought energies that surrounds every person, which emanates the mood of that person.

She said again that her body just didn't feel right; I asked her if she wanted me to take her to the doctor. **"No, I'll be alright,"** she said like always, I believed she had really given up on life. She became very still and silent, **sitting in her recliner chair, she asked me again if God was punishing her.** I explained that **God doesn't punish** anyone, and that we create our own reality by what we choose to believe, think, feel and act on. Thought is the greatest power of all. Out of our ignorance and violation of Spirit (God) Universal Laws, we suffer.

We are governed by your thoughts that create your own world, the physical as well as nonphysical. Through our thought, we reap what we sow; it's the Law of Attraction (cause and effect or action and reaction). We are all vibrating on different levels of consciousness. Depending on

110

what's really in our subconscious mind, we manifest our beliefs sooner or later. She reaped what she sowed. Energy follows thoughts. Her body conditions and life were showing where her unconscious was vibrating all of her life.

KNOW, TRUST AND LOVE ALL ASPECT OF YOUR DIVINE WHOLE SELF!

"In that they show the work of the law written in their hearts, their conscience bearing witness, and their thoughts alternately accusing or else defending them."   -Romans 2:15

After helping her pack for her vacation, she once again tried to give me her sacred quilt; I refused again, she walked me to the elevator and made a tight fist, **ensuring me she was strong and alright.** A few weeks prior, **she had fallen** in her building stairwell and hurt her wrist. Truly, she was reaping what she had sown **VICTIM CONSCIOUSNESS.** Her body conditions were showing her true feelings about herself and her life!

"God cares for our body and soul, healing every kind of disease and sickness."   -Matthew 9:3

From my own experience of listening and observing most religious people that go to church to me it like going to a **slaughterhouse** because most of the time they kill the **TRUE GOD** Spirit within us. Yes! They pretend to serve a good purpose with its **fake sister and brotherhood.** They should be teaching people to **KNOW ENERGETICALLY** and inner and over-stand their **GOD GODDESS SELF WITHIN.** Most people are under the illusion of feelings like a sinner, unloved, loneliness, inferiority and a lack of true faith, courage, not willing to

trust   their Christ self within and be **responsible or**

accountable for what they **keep creating**. In addition, we feel hurt, confused, unhappy, inadequate, Yes! Most churches pretend to do some good, such as giving out unhealthy food that the city provided and drawing people in through church-owned daycare centers and all kind of socializing, other trappings now rap singing events, competitions, basketball and football leagues etc. to draw more youth into churches To me for most people church is like a club for entertaining for escapism, psychologically the reverend or pastors becomes their father/mother figure or their man or women, people feel they need some type of authority figure (SLAVERY) over them. I choose a nightclub for my entertaining; some people choose the church or both. VICTIMS are VOLUNTEERS.

"On the cross Jesus cried, 'Eli, Eli lama sabachthani?' that is, 'My God, my God, why has thou forsaken me?'"   –Matthew27:46

Metaphysically, sabachthani is the cry of the soul at the darkest hour of crucifixion. When the sensual is passing away, it seems as though man is giving up all his life, including every good. The sensual looms so large at this hour that, for the time being, it shuts God from the consciousness of the individual who is going through the experience. But God never forsakes his children; there can be no real separation from the divine, and a glorious resurrection into a greater degree of spiritual life than was ever realized before always follows each letting go of the old. Metaphysical Bible Dictionary by Unity (page 562)

Check out: Share International NY.www.share-international.us/ne. 877-495-774

Chapter 22
Home Going

June 5, 2002, a beautiful, warm, bright and sunny morning, was when I found out Magnolia was in **Intensive Care** at Montefiore Hospital, as I was getting dressed to go visit her **I received a call from the doctor,** asking permission to do a specific procedure. I gave my okay as long as they assured me they **wouldn't operate on her or put her on life support.** She had made it very clear that she didn't want that under any circumstance. She wanted to make her transition with some dignity. When I arrived at the hospital the Intensive Care staff told me to wait until the doctors were finished working on her. Delores and a friend came later some more of her church members. After we waited an hour in the waiting area, the doctor came out and told us she was in critical condition and wasn't going to last much longer. He added that he didn't know how she lasted that long, because most of all of her organs were destroyed.

When we all went in to see her, I became **upset and angry** because she was **hooked up to a life support machine,** but my **higher self** said at this point it didn't matter. **We** surrounded her bed, I started caressing her forehead. The church member wanted us all to hold hands while the Deacon said a prayer I really didn't want to but, I did it for her; it's what she was about. I was feeling all kinds of emotions: first hurt, followed by anger, guilt, abandonment, and fear. I was angry because her **false religious teachings** contributed to her condition that she **consented to.** She had never learned who she truly was and how to heal her **wounded inner child** and how to **forgive herself and others, which is easier said than done! (I know!)**

"My people are destroyed for their lack of knowledge." -Hosea 4:6 (True knowledge and inner and over standing) R.W.

113

I became quiet, wondering whether I had did all I could to help deprogram her out of the false illusion she was in.   **A** trance that so many people don't realize they're in. Believe me, I know change is scary and most of the time painful. I felt abandoned because she was leaving me on this physical plane. I felt fearful, wondering how I would feel when the truth sinks in that her physical presence is gone. Still standing there caressing her forehead, a sense of peace came over me. Then I realized her Spirit had already left the body and was hovering on the right side corner of the ceiling. I started communicating with her Spirit, telepathically telling her to leave and that I'll be alright. Then the monitors attached to her stopped blinking and beeping, I felt numb all over. I guess at that point I didn't know what I was feeling again. I couldn't hold back the tears. Her church member tried to console me, I am grateful to them for theirs effort. which only aggravated me as I felt her church's teachings were the main cause for most of her imbalances.

My inner Spirit said, "Just breathe deeply, relax, get centered and grounded and feel all the hurt and anger to the fullest, and then release it." It was consuming me to the point that I wanted to curse those church people out, because they just kept perpetrating misrepresentations of the truth. They thought I was hurting and crying because she had lost her life (died). In reality, I was happy she made her transition because I knew she had never really lived her own life, experiencing own her mistakes and learning and growing from them for her own evolution instead of someone else's (PARENTS MISTAKES, and FALSE NEGATIVE PROGRAMMING)

They all left me alone in the room with her to say my goodbye. About twenty minutes I just reflected on some of our good times together. When I left her room **Delores** was the only one still in the waiting room. In an attempt to console me she said, "Let's get something to drink tea or coffee?" So, we went to a restaurant across from the hospital and talked about our godmother's (so-called) life. She was surprised that I felt happy and sad about her transition; I really knew her pain, suffering, physical and mental agony and she suffered in silence like most people. I couldn't inner/over-stand how her being in a congregation for about fifty years or more that professed knowledge about the Creator they called God, no one saw or felt her emotional and mental pain, her fear of living and dying. No one I knew of tried to help her face and release the negative spirits or demons inside her that were created by her false fears, anger, resentments, jealousy, no self-love, false beliefs, low frequency etc. Did anyone really knew or cared to help her with her guilt and her misinterpretation that she was born in sin (REALLY IGNROANCE) which made her feel more unworthy and she worried that the Devil was trying to destroy her body, or that she was going to die and go to Hell. She didn't realize she was already there (just a state of mind, consciousness)!

In 1999, I was told Pope John Paul II said on television that there's no such place as Hell, that Hell is a state of mind. (Read Matthew 6:1-8) Magnolia thought she needed the external approval; she was unable to recognize and appreciate her own worth, (Like most of us).She found fault in others if they didn't comply with or accept what she valued and believed for example her religion. She made comments about how others lived their lives and blamed others unconsciously for refusing to accept responsibility they created in their life. She couldn't see she was in the same boat, by what she had chosen to accept and believe. (Believing, is not knowing) She was really feeling loneliness most of her life, even in a crowd. She unconsciously pitied herself, and created and accepted sickness, it gave her a false feeling of value by being sick, she would get attention, sympathy from others and they would be motivated to show her love. She used the church to MASK

115

(hide) her feelings of inferiority, loneliness, self-hatred, no self -worth, the list goes on.

"To grow is necessary, to outgrow is necessary, and to leave behind the good for the sake of the better is necessary" -Sri Nisargadatta Maharaj

After leaving the hospital, I never viewed Magnolia's body again. For me the only thing that's dead is a dead mind. Sad to say, but that's a lot of people walking around.

"Awake thou that sleeper and arise from the dead and Christ shall give thee light [truth)   -Ephesians: 5:14

"But the Spirit explicitly says that later times some will fall away from the (true) Faith paying attention to deceitful Spirits and doctrines of demons."   -1- Timothy 4:1

I used the dis-ease to wake-up to my own truth and empowerment realizing it was within me all the time! My godmother was like millions of people, governed by ideas, opinions, and religious beliefs dating back thousands of years, most of which have been misinterpreted or are absolutely false.   (The dead still rule.)

"According to your faith is it done unto you."   -Matthew 9:29

It's law! It doesn't matter whether you call yourself Catholic, Jew, Protestant, Christian, Seventh Day Adventist, Buddhist, Baptist, Hindu, Jehovah's Witness, Heathen, etc.

"Great peace has they which love thy law and nothing shall offend them."   -Psalms 119:165

"Let the words of my mouth [your thoughts, mental images] and the meditations of my heart [your feeling, nature, emotions] are acceptable in thy sight, O Lord [the law of your subconscious mind], my strength, and my redeemer [the power and wisdom of your subconscious mind that can redeem you from sickness, bondage, and misery]." -J. Murphy

The (so-called) Devil gets blamed for everything.

When are we going to take responsibility for all that we create that which we don't like or want?

Most so-called Reverends, Popes, Pastors, Bishops, and Elders are using basic psychology in their sermons, and they are teaching some basic universal laws. However, they still perpetuate the false religious dogma too, and dependence. It's like having an apple with rotten spot, when you cut out the rotten spot, you only eat what is good. Using basic common sense make the decision for yourself what is right, wrong or appropriate; you don't have to eat the whole apple.

June 10, 2002 was my godmother's home going (funeral). My daughter Adrienne was by my side. She knew how much Magnolia meant to me. The service was held at her church, in Harlem, most of the people who attended were members, the church being her only so-called life. I listened to what some of them had to say, talking as if they really knew her.   I got very upset and angry; I couldn't take it anymore. The preacher talked nonsense about how we all loved her but God loved her more, insinuating that their GOD caused her death; I walked out before the service was over. While sitting in the lobby crying a warm compassionate church member tried to console me, she put her arms around me; her energy felt good. I asked if there was a restroom I could use and she took me to one behind the reception desk, another church member who saw us got very upset with the fact that I was about to use the Pastor's personal lavatory, but the first lady said, "Please, just go ahead; it's alright." When I was inside I looked around and thought what the problem is? It's just another restroom! I just wanted to get the hell out of that so-called house of God.

(Your body is the living temple)

"The most high dwelleth not in temples made with hands   -Acts 7:48

LOVE AND TRUST YOUR DIVINE SOURCE WITHIN YOU!
Known by many names

Church of Christ - Spiritual consciousness first individual then collective, In the general usage, the word church applies to persons who have been "born anew" (John 3:3) through the quickening power of the word, gathered together in one body, their union being typified by the human body. Jesus never organized a church on earth; neither did He authorize anyone else to do so. He said to Peter, "Upon this rock I will build my church" (Matthew 16:18). He did not tell Peter that he was to be the head of the church, with a line of popes to follow. He said, "I will build my church" (ecclesia, "assembly," or called-out ones). Jesus is still the head of His "assembly," and its only organization is in Spirit. He gave but one guide, one source from which His followers should receive their inspiration: "The Holy Spirit, whom the Father will send in my name, he shall teach you all things, and bring to your remembrance all that I said unto you." (Read John 14:26) - (Charles Fillmore (page 37)

The day after the funeral, when I went to Magnolia's apartment for the first time since her transition, I got off the train at the Jackson Avenue stop on Westchester Avenue. As usual, I stopped at the fruit and vegetable market to buy some flowers, thinking I'd give them to her sister-in-law, Pat. From the first time I met her and her husband Magnolia brother Tom, I liked them and fell in love with their Spirit

118

but to my amazement for the first time the market had no flowers at all! I continued to her apartment, dreading to go inside, knowing she wouldn't be there. When I arrival I found the apartment in disarray. Her brother and his wife, their sisters and her son (let's call him) Greg were there I talked with them for a half hour, and then in private with her brother, I revealed to him things that had deeply hurt her. All her life, he understood and identified with some of her pain because he too had experienced similar hurts in his childhood.

Later, back in the living room his wife Pat tried to make small talk about how Magnolia would call from New York to Georgia and would disguise her voice asking to speak to her brother. Pat said she was always joking like that, but I knew better she only wanted to speak with her brother, not that her sister in law had done something bad to her, but because she was jealous of her, Magnolia was jealous of how well her brother treated her, unlike how her own husband had treated her by always placing his mother and sister before her. When I shared with everyone there that I was writing this book and that she inspired me to tell her story too, I felt the energy in the room drop, I guess they were wondering what Magnolia had said about them. As I prepared to leave Magnolia apartment I looked around the living room the pictures, the large teddy bear etc. and the plaque I had just given her were all gone. I felt a little empty and hurt. The reality hit me that this was it. She's not in the physical any longer; she's vibrating on another level of dimension! (in my house there are many rooms)

Tom gave me a few things of hers, for which I am grateful for having, now I wanted to the quilt, her brother told me one of their sister took it already, he said "trying to get it back would be a problem." So I let that go and learned a powerful lesson: The next time someone dear to my heart wants to give me something that's dear to their heart before they make their transition (die), I will accept it!

Greg   Magnolia son walked me to the train; we talked about his early life with his adoptive mother (Magnolia who was biologically his aunt). After my godmother's transition, I acquired a lot more details about life. I understood his life with her became increasingly difficult as he aged. She did the best she knew how. She thought the only thing good and valuable she had to give him was what was given or taught to her - the book called the Bible and her religious   dogma, indoctrination (programming); she had no sense of real self, her SOUL which is in the heart center. The world has a fondness for those who conform to its false values. All Greg really wanted from her was a mother LOVE in its TRUEST FORM. WE can live brain dead, but not heart for long.

ENTER INTO YOUR SHADOW SIDE THAT ONLY IDENIFY WITH YOUR FALSE EGO OF FEAR, LOVE IT AND YOU CONQUER IT.

BREAK THE EGG SHELL AND COME OUT NOW!

"Limited thoughts create limited people."

"For the Lord giveth wisdom. Out of his/her mouth cometh knowledge and understanding, Meditate on the truth. -Proverbs 2:6

Chapter 23
Harmony Leads To Love,
Which Is Everything

Magnolia adopted Greg when he was very young, one of her sister's son; she tried her best to be a good mother without really knowing how to express real love, nurturing, or inner and over-standing who he is and his soul purpose for being on earth at this time, because she didn't know herself. As Greg grew older their relationship became more difficult. She just didn't understand that he was trying to find his own identity and life purpose. She only knew conformity, which is what she had been accustomed to. It takes a brave person not to conform, to go against the grain to find their SOUL PATH, because it means you may have to stand alone, and most people are afraid to stand alone by their own faith and convictions. He didn't want to hear that same old false religious dogma and live a mundane existence like her and those who are still in that mind-set. After he became an adult, he moved to another state, got married, and had two beautiful daughters. Their relationship worsened over the years (but that's his story to tell).

Greg's marriage didn't last long. There were issues from the beginning; both just couldn't take it any longer. Most of us learn from our parents, family members, and peers to settle for less in life, to conform (sheep follower) like the majority of people. An example, to stay in a marriage or relationship when it has run its course, or to just get married to "escape" feeling that void deep inside of our self. Like myself, I got married to escape my parents; whereas, some people get married to please their parents. Be the LION THAT YOU ARE!

"Sow a thought, reap an act; sow an act, reap a habit; sow a habit, reap a character; sow a character, reap a destiny."
-Chinese Proverb

"Trust in the lord [law] with all your heart, and do not lean on your own understanding. In all your ways acknowledge the law and it will make your path straight."-Proverbs 3:5-6

Exercise 1
Practice being silence, sit very still, hands on thighs, palms up, or lay down flat, arms straight, palms facing up or placed over your heart chakra center. Breathe deeply from your diaphragm for about three minutes, (expand the chest while filling yourself with chi - energy). While relaxing, close your eyes then go into the silence and clear all thoughts. When thoughts come, don't focus on them; just let them pass.

Now, while you hold your breath, mentally count from one to three or one to ten (whatever is most comfortable), then exhale, releasing all excess chi While you do this, focus on the third eye, the pituitary gland in the middle of the forehead (just above heart chakra in your chest, a little to the left of center), or focus on the solar plexus chakra above the navel. Place your left hand on one of these areas, standing or sitting, and, if you are sitting, place your right hand behind your body in the same area (or as close to it as you comfortably can), palms facing the body. Go deeper inside of yourself, Now ask yourself any question about your

Life and listen with your heart (not your mind). You may see an image or symbol, hear a voice, or have a thought or feeling, then or later. Ask your Spirit what these images means to you.

Exercise II
Go within yourself, make sure your spine is always straight, do deep breathing, relax, and clear your mind and align your HEART with your SPIRIT, then visualize what you desire one thing at a time, or if they relate to each other, write it

down nine or twenty-one times on a piece of paper every day. Even say it out loud to yourself and feel it until you manifest what you desire in divine order. Examples: I am healthy now! I am wealthy, rich, and successful now! My perfect spiritual partner is with me now! Then, give thanks for it in the present and LET IT GO! IN DIVINE ORDER!

Breathe deeply, relax, close your eyes, visualize and feel what you want and go within yourself, and place your hand on your heart. Ask the universe what is rightfully yours by Divine Law. See what feelings come up and write your own affirmation.

FIND YOUR OWN TRUTH! WITH IN YOU

Don't keep believing in the DECEPTION. (Do your research) watch the movie: INCEPTION

OPEN YOUR MIND AND HEART YOU HAVE THE DIVINE POWER TO CREATE YOUR OWN REALITY.

Chapter 24
Full Circle

While waiting on the platform for the train to return to my apartment, I started thinking about the fruit market having no flowers; **I'm still bewildered.** Then all of a sudden I became engulfed with this warm, peaceful energy, I felt this mighty presence saying, **"There were no flowers today to let you know that you already gave them to her when it really mattered. They're in her heart,"** and I felt her smiling.

I knew in that instant that I had evolved a little more. I am open to the universe and over-stand so much more because of my out-of-body experience. I am not afraid of TRANSITING/DYING or of the experience of my loved ones dying, although it still hurts. Parenting is one of the hardest (challenging) assignments on Earth because most people weren't taught how to be truly loving, nurturing and how to inner and over-standing themselves or their children.

Dysfunctional people, in most cases, raise dysfunctional children in some way. Their wounds never heal, so they perpetuate the dysfunctional mindset (pattern) in some form or another. Whether a parent or not, I encourage you to fill in the blanks on the next page not to hurt or judge anyone, but to heal, forgive and release the wounds and being whole.

On the next page, get relaxed, breathe deeply from the diaphragm three times, each time exhaling slowly, and remain quiet and still for a few minutes before proceeding answering the questions.

BE TRULY HONEST WITH YOURSELF FIRST!

1. What was the most important thing I felt I needed as a child and didn't get?

_____

_____

_____

2. Why I think I didn't get it?

_____

_____

_____

3. How would I have felt if I had received it?

_____

_____

4. What would I have said or done as a child if I could have, and to whom?

_____

5. What six major things did I learn from my childhood experience, positive or negative?

_____

_____

_____

6. Why I think I chose my parents?

_____

125

_____

_____

7. What do I really value in yourself and others?

_____

_____

_____

8. Who am I? (Don't include things like "I am a parent, a wife, a sister, a brother, husband, a professional, etc.")

_____

_____

_____

9. How do I feel about my life at this moment?

_____

_____

_____

10. Why do I feel this way?

_____

_____

_____

11. How can I change this and by when?

_____

_____

_____

12. What do I truly believe would make me happy or happier and bring me JOY?

_____

_____

_____

13. How do I feed my spirit and soul?

_____

_____

_____

14. How can I awaken to my Divine self and power?

_____

_____

_____

Make Something Profound and Great Happen To Help Humanity!
Awake out of Race Consciousness into The Creator (God) **Higher**

Consciousness!

Race Consciousness - The human race has formed laws of physical birth and death, laws of sickness and physical inability, laws making food the source of bodily existence, laws of mind that recognize no other source of existence except the physical. The sum total of these laws is from a race consciousness separate from and independent of creative Mind. When creative Mind sought to help men spiritually, the mind of the flesh opposed it and made every effort to solve its problem in its own way. The great need of the human family is mind control. Jesus showed us that mastery is attained through realization of the power of Spirit.   -Charles Fillmore (page 162)

Proselyte - one who has turned away from the old set of religious forms and ceremonies and realized truth for him/herself.   -C. Fillmore (page 157)

My highest growth lesson was remembering who I really AM! You don't need to seek enlightenment; you just need to open yourself up to what's really inside – and just BE! Detach from the negative illusions out there!

My experiences with Magnolia continue for the last few years, I really thought I was teaching her. Now I realize she was teaching me - encouraging, inspiring, and supporting me in every aspect of my life, all the time letting me know I was on **MY RIGHT PATH.** She mirrored to me what was wrong with her belief system and the way she lived her life (or rather, didn't live).
YOUR GREATEST TEACHER is the HOLY SPIRIT /MOTHER (NOT GHOST) GODDESS/GOD WITHIN YOU.

"The Holy Spirit, whom the Father (Mother) will send in thy name, shall teach you all things and bring to your remembrance all that I say unto you."   -John 14:26

Magnolia didn't to live not able to care for herself and she was afraid to make her transition too. She forgot like most of us, it is not a bad process or an ending; it's a continuing to another level of vibration called the Spirit realm (invisible). She didn't want some medical system to help keep her here suffering just to make more money especially since her body had deteriorated over the years and the same thing happened to her mother whose suffering she observed that frighten her more. When she couldn't care for herself any longer, **she was not selfish to continue to hold on, and I knew I had to be selfless to release her with dignity.** She finally got something she wanted for herself, just for herself. **She was hospitalized on Tuesday and Transition, (died) gone back home the next day.**

I am so happy, that she finally got what she wanted, at the end of this physical challenge, **just a new beginning.** I value my life and everyone else even more now. I make an **effort** to live my life to the fullest every day, taking nothing for granted anymore. **I realize that the most valuable thing we have is our Soul (consciousness) and that determines what level where we go after we leave the body. I believe she is on a level in Spirit, learning (remembering) the truth about her true self and what she didn't tap into on the physical level through Spirit while she was here because of her false taught beliefs. Her UNCONSCIOUS was filled with fear, doubt, confusion, hurt, self-hatred and more. (Wow)!!!**

(You get the picture.) Some medical systems, like politics, most educational systems and especially religion, keep us ignorant of our authentic self. It's about the big bucks they get. Read "The Art of Seduction" by Robert Greene, and "Coercion: Why We Listen to What They Say" by Douglas Rushkoff, watch documentary SICKO movie by Michael Moore.

2003, I heard a Reverend on a cablevision program preaching and saying that most high school students cannot name ten presidents and the year they served. I am over **sixty years of age;** I cannot and care not to learn either. **What's the point,** if you don't know your **own true self** first which is ENERGY and how your mind, body, spirit, and soul operate and are essentially important...or should! They teach us to believe in the religious dogma, or what someone else says is truth, and become co-dependent. The only power politicians, religion, or anyone has over us is the power we give up to them. Religion has not ever saved anyone; it's your true faith. Because what you put out into the universe returns sooner or later, this is **UNIVERSAL LAWS.** (Read Timothy 4:1-4)

"**Anointed by Yahweh (God) – one who is conscious of the real spiritual outpouring from the source of his being; a consecrated person.**" -Luke 4:18

About a week after the **funeral, Ann** called me and said, "**Mother Salem** (Magnolia) loved me **but she praised you!**" I believe when my godmother had her **miscarriage, I was that Spirit intended to come through, but didn't because of what she had impressed in her subconscious mind as a young girl out of her ignorance.** That level of consciousness caused the miscarriage that resulted in her having a **hysterectomy.** Our bond was still strong enough to draw us back together to give each other what we needed. **I am the daughter she wanted, and she will always be one of the mothers I needed.**

Thank you, God-mamma, for teaching me to give up the lesser **Man-made religion**, for the **greater Soul Realization/Universal consciousness**.

There are many levels of consciousness: the physical, astral, causal, and mental.

"I will instruct you   -Psalms 32:8

"**They show that what the law requires is written on their hearts, to which their own conscience also bears witness.**"
-Romans 2:15

On February 7, 2002, one of my daughter's co-worker's infant died (transition). Tajiri was a beautiful twelve-week and three-day old baby boy with a loving Spirit. I met my daughter Adrienne and the mother of the baby at Lincoln Hospital. I never imagined I would ever be holding a lifeless baby's body in my arms without emotionally falling apart with grief. Even she surprised me; we were both strong and courageous. Oh yes! We shared some tears, had deep compassion and concerns for the mother of this highly evolve spirit, I met his mother and him for the first time that day. Tajiri was a gift and a special soul that came for a short stay, I don't know or understand what all the lessons, gifts and challenges he came here to offer the people's lives he touched. I am so grateful for that gift that I was allowed to experience through his spirit and soul. It confirmed my belief in my chosen spiritual path for my life that I am in the right consciousness path, that the physical body is temporary (take care of it) and not to take life for granted or too serious. What is really important in our lives is our Soul; it's the only valuable essence of yourself you take with you through your transition. Your soul is the essences of unconditional love that you share with yourself and with others, that can help change someone's life for the betterment and world peace.

What do I REALLY TRULY VALUE and WHY?

What's my INTENTION, What will be my DIVINE LEGACY?

It's not important how long you live; it's the purpose you served and the quality of how you live and died (leave here). I could still feel his presence in the hospital room. I felt a sense of peace, love, and felt he was in a good place in consciousness, back into the Spirit realm. I was being prepared to handle my **godmother's transition that same year. Thank you, Tajiri!**

The **consistent practice of meditation brings great healing benefits: mental, physical, and spiritual.** It calms the mind, along with centering and relaxing the body. This allows us to reach a deeper connection with our inner self, the God within - just by being, **listening, trusting, and obeying.**

"Death is not the greatest loss; it's what dies inside of us while we live." -unknown

Exercise 111

Sit in a lotus position on the floor. If this is not comfortable for you, sit in a chair with your back straight and feet placed flat on the floor, wear comfortable and neutral colored clothing, always align your heart with spirit. Place your hands on your thighs, palms facing up or first three fingertips together visualize gold light. You may tense and relax every part of your body, from toe to head. Breathe in slowly and deeply, and try to establish a regular rhythm. Feel how your abdomen rises and falls as you inhale and exhale by focusing on your breathing and just above your third eye slightly to the right side. This is one of the ways you can begin to enter a meditative state of mind.

I now wake up almost every day feeling like I just came out of heaven a state of consciousness. I don't really want to come out of that state of mind, to see the illusion we accepted as real. I feel more alive than ever before in that state of mind thanking the Creator for allowing me to truly live as long as I am alive. Feeling loving, joyous, peaceful, healthy, wealthy, powerful, and teachable and ever changing, I continuously asking how I can be of service today, and how I can help humanity to get back to living in harmony and make a positive difference during this short time, I am passing through earth. That's why this book was channeled through me to be of some real help to humanity.

And with all of your positive energy and support we will manifest a Self-Awareness Center (the building) very soon!

On January 1, 1998, between 12:00 am Or 1:00 am, I was inspired to look out my kitchen window (on the first floor side of my building) after it had snowed. I saw in large print these words written in the snow: (what we call) "Happy New Year to all," "Love one another," "Be good to each other." I called my son; Clifford so read it he did and he smiled.

The next morning, the snow had melted and the words were gone, but I will never forget them. They were engraved in my heart. I asked around the neighborhood to find out who wrote it, no one knew, nor had anyone else seen the writing. However that night, that moment was like magic for me. I learned to give when I thought I had so little or nothing to give. I give of myself, which in essence is how I became a true giver not expecting (no false Ego) anything in return from anyone. The universe pays all deeds good (positive) or bad (negative). It's just a matter of when and how.

There was something very peaceful and loving in the air that I believe is always there. We get so caught up in the material world that we cover it up and lose sight of what's authentic. It's never too late to change your life because every day is a miracle and YOU are that miracle. There is nothing in the entire world greater than freedom of your soul and mind to think for yourself and be your Divine Self.

"It doesn't pay to stay stuck in the past; there is NO FUTRUE or NOW in it."
(Live in the moment and be GRACEFUL)
-R.W.

"Do not call to mind the former things or ponder things of past. Behold, I will do something new. Now it will spring forth; will you not be aware of it? I will even make a roadway in the wilderness, rivers in the desert."   -Isaiah 43:18-19

Savior - The Christ Mind is our Savior; through the Christ Mind we find salvation from poverty, sickness, sin, and death. - (Charles Fillmore (page 173)

Choose all the positive and good things you need and deserve in divine order. Learn to live in the present moment. Choose integrity, truth love, honesty, compassion, courage, peace, health, wealth, wholeness, non-attachment, non-compliance for freedom of mind and Soul. Don't be afraid of taking baby steps upward and forward; be afraid of standing still or going in the same circles seeking the false illusion.

ALL DIVINE SOULS ARE ONE IN THE MIND OF GOD!

Help the AUTHOR to continue learning, growing spiritual and helping everyone who are ready.

All LOVE OFFERING (ENERDY EXCHANGE) ARE APPRRCAITED

PLEASE! Would You Help!!! And post all positive comments regarding her books on her website chakraspectrums.com (paypal), Facebook, Amazon (E-Book), Createspace or any other post.

Divine Guidance

These are the authors and book titles, just to name a few, that the True Spirit guided me to read, study, examine and meditate on. I share them with you to expand your mind to explore and reconnect to the True Divine Spirit.

Mass Control: Engineering Human Consciousness by-Jim Keith, Ron Amitron: Stargates-Timelines-Cloning & YOU, Deepak Chopra and Dr. Sebi - herbalist, Joseph Campbell, John H. Clarke (a black historian), Caroline Myss, The Bhagavad-Gita, Paramahansa Yogananda, Black Labor, White Wealth by Claude Anderson, Dr. Cornel West –The Rich and the rest of us, Develop Your Psychic Abilities by Litany Burns, Know Thyself by Sathya Sai Baba, The Millionaire Moses by- Catherine Ponder, Homecoming by John Bradshaw, Spiritual Growth by Sanaya Roman, Deceptions and Myths of the Bible by Lloyd Graham.

The Breath and what is Spirit and Soul? by Malachi Z. Yoke-el, Know Thyself by Naim Akbar, Blueprint for Black Power by Dr. Amos Wilson, The Kybalion Philosophy by Hermetic, The Life and Teachings of the Masters of the Far East 1-6 by Baird T. Spalding, Bringers of the Dawn by Barbara Marciniak, You Are Becoming a Galactic Human by Virginia Essene and Cheldon Nidle, The Mystic Path to Cosmic Power by- Vernon Howard, The Gods of Egyptians by E. A. Wallis Budge, It's Not What You're Eating, It's What's Eating You by Janet Greeson, P.H.D. The Millionaire Moses by- Catherine Ponder.

David Icke.com and listen to "Piercing the Illusion," a collection by Jonathan Parker and "Deadly Deception," the proof that sex and HIV absolutely do not cause AIDS by Robert E.

Willner, M.D., PhD. The Mis- Education of the Negro by Carter G. Woodson's, Edgar Cayce's Millennium Prophecies by Mark Thurston, Ph.D.'s, "Meditation: the First and Last Freedom" by Osho, Resurrection by- Neville, Traditional African Religion by Geoffrey Parrinder's, and Tree of Life Meditation System by Ra Un Nefer Amen, Total self Confidence- Dr. Robert Anthony, When things fall apart by- Pema Chodron, Architects of Mind Control by- Michael Tsarion, Alchemy of Nine Dimensions by- Barbara HandClow with Gerry Clow, Bashar-Trick of negative belief, Alan Watts- Stop COMPETING with yourself.

Re-examine all you have been taught, heard or seen. Dismiss what Doesn't Serve your SOUL /CHRIST CONSCIOUSNESS THE LEADER YOU WERE SEEKING IS YOU!

REVELATION IS NOW!

R-EVOLUTION IS NOW!!!!

CONTEST SUGGESTION TITLES

1. Suffering and Dying From Ignorance

2. Piercing the Illusions

3. The Key to Having Everything You Need

4. God's Truth, Will Set You Free

5. Universal Laws is "Cause and Effect"

6. Know Thy True Goddess/ Godself

7. You Got The Power!

8. My Journey through the Darkness into the Light (Truth)

9. God's Truth or Man's Religion

10. You Are the Key to Open Any Door

11. Karma, We Reap What We Sow

12. The Power within you - (No Excuses)

13. The Way Out is By Going Within

14. Lost Confused Souls

15. The Truth Will Let You See, the Seed of

The Creator Is You

16. No More Lies or Deceptions

17. Bondage or Freedom!

18. Who Is Really Controlling Your Reality

Contest Rules: -Pick one of the above titles that you think I would have selected for this book and forward your selection to the following email address: chakraspectrums@netzero.net

-One out of the first 50 selections with the correct title will receive $500.00
Visit website: chakraspectrums.com /youtube/facebook

HER 2 NEWEST BOOKS ARE AVAILABLE NOW-

ASCENSION, SOUL REVRIEVAL, RESURRECTION # 1 and 2.

HER FOURTH BOOK TITLE "WHY' THE END OF 2015

JUST A FEW BOOK COMMENTS

"The Book Without a Name is a practical empowering book based on Rose's true life experiences for healing on all levels, for personal growth and transformation. It is easy to inner/overstand how to apply universal laws and how you can change your life forever. From reading this book she was initiated from within and from above. She went though many stages of transformation for Ascension and development, to develop her Higher Spiritual Gifts, For Rite of Passage.

-Dr. John Bolling, MD. Child psychiatrist, Author and lecturer

Hi! Rose Great book! And great title Thank for giving us the opportunity to share your work with our readers.
--Inner Realm magazine

Rose shares some of her personal and family life experiences to illustrate the illusion or disillusion people were in. This was something that frustrated the many of them were stuck in religious rut and didn't know it or how to get out of it. Her book really shows that she is living from a higher self and is on a mission to help as many people as she can. A goal I would say is well on her way toward achieving. Rose suggests ways to determine your life purpose, ways to make contact with GOD through meditation and provides reference books to help you progress on your spiritual path. I found the book inspiring because it validated again things that Saints, Sages, Gurus and other Masters have said for thousands of years. Seek GOD within you with your whole heart and Soul and you will find true happiness and love. I recommend reading this book because of its inspiring message that will uplift your spirit, especially one part of the book which brought tears to my eyes. I would like to THANK YOU ROSE for being yet another beacon of light sent by GOD. Many Blessings and keep up the good work. -   -Michael Sassano Yoga Instructor

I think this is the first book, I read that really helped me begin my transformation from being unhappy and feeling helpless was this wonderful book by, Rose Whaley- The Book Without a Name: You Read it You Name It. While I read this, I truly became transformed and this sister spoke to me so clearly. This is the story of how Sister Rose Whaley transformed her life, healed herself from cancer, released herself from an abusive relationship and manifested the happy, faithful, loving being that she has always been! This is an empowering read! S O U L I S T I C H E A L I N G.COM –from California

Rose Whaley's experiences in her book are truly tools for all of us. Her life journey has been food for thought for all our Souls. Anyone who holds this book in their hands will feel truth, honesty, love and good will. God gave us this wonderful teacher at this now crucial time. - Eve Kerwin Shamanic Healer and Channeler Author of: The Awakening

Hi GODDESS ROSE!
THANK YOU! THANKYOU! There is NO WORDS to DESCRIBE An EYE OPENING EMPOWERING BOOK LIKE YOURS.   - From-Spain- Armando

The Book Without A name –Is just what we need to cause all of us to pause and examine ourselves. Thank you for being the channel through which it was allowed to flow. I was initially attracted to the cover to which I was drawn as if by a magnet. The colors and designs are simply magnificent! Upon closer examination, I discovered that the title "A Book Without A Name," coupled with the opportunity being given to the reader to read it and name it, is an idea that could only come from Spirit. It is absolutely unique. At this point my curiosity is at its peak and there is no way that I could resist exploring the contents and needless to say, by this time I was hooked. I did not stop until I had read the entire book and what a reward!! The manner in which you present the story of your life with deep insight, reading each experience and seeing it as part of a "BIGGER PICTURE," that is designed for the purpose of promoting spiritual unfoldment and contributing to the evolution, not only in your life, but also in the lives of those of us who are a part of your life and ultimately the entire planet, is simply unprecedented. Especially powerful is the emphasis on demonstrating Metaphysical /Spiritual/ Universal Truths, showing that they are supported by and in agreement with quotes taken from the widely accepted "King James" version of the bible. This is truly a stroke of genius that could only have flowed through you directly from the "SOURCE. "Rose, this book is truly a master piece and its reaching the public at this time is perfect! Thank you for answering the call to be that clear channel that brings this light into our planet. Much Love and Many Blessing   -Reverend Susie B. Williams Director

Rose book! Won the 2007 Self-Publishing Symposium S'INDIE AWARDS for TRAILBLAZER / Two books signing at Barns & Nobles in NY

Congratulation on writing your book, I enjoy reading and marveled at your ability to lay bare so many personal aspects of your life. Of course it is clear you did this in the interest of helping others. The book makes one want to look closely at the situations in life that we still cling to and how we are shaped by circumstances. It is often easier to do something once you see someone else do it. This is the effect that it had on me and I believe others will feel the same. That you were able to overcome so much adversity will be shining examples to anyone who reads and understands your book. The book reads exactly the way you sound when you have your seminars. What a pleasure. Look forward to your next book.-Yours Truly- Ann Sealy/ Entrepreneur, Activist, Designer/ Seamstress

Reading your book was like peeking into the universe and seeing the answers. I was so overwhelmed at the events in your life that were similar to my life. I love the word "OVERSTAND" I now "over-stand" the reason that everything that happen to me was for me to learn a lesson. A lesson that I will share with others, I Thank you for having the COURGAGE to write and publish your book, you have inspired me to do the same. I now have much to draw from.

- Much Love, Cheryl

First, I have to say that I am soooooo blessed that the Creator has brought you into my life!!! You have been such a foundation in my spiritual growth, and for that I am truly graceful!! Rose this book is going to be such a blessing to so many people. Your life story has always been so amazing and so inspiring to me. To see it in print, it speaks volumes about how much we truly have control of our lives by using the laws of attraction. I love the way you spoke in the book. I am looking forward to your parenting book so I can over-stand (smile) being a better parent to Zuri. I love you girl!!! Growing in the spirit daily!   Icy Barzey -an-Dietitian and Entrepreneur

YOUR BOOK, I must say that you are radiant, full of life and power. I can't explain what your energy has done for me. I hear in your voice a person that is honest and intelligence established beyond the system of educations. You have the gift of black women the Creator of all men. Love begins with women like you. It is this courage that has sustained countless children. Thank you for sharing your true beauty with me. Kevin R. Smith –Area Director- ClubZ Tutoring Services

Thank you for writing such an awe inspiring book. It was such a pleasure to, and I've recommended your book to so many people and will continue to do so. I am now reading it again. Who you are now is so far removed from what you were then that one would never believe that such experiences were yours if you had not written your book. Kudos to you and GOD BLESS YOU!   -Y. Lasky

This book was an easy read and is a great testament to the human spirit and what one can achieve if one truly seeks the GOD within us all Rose Whaley not only sought GOD but actually made contact with her in the process. She healed herself at not only a spiritual level but at a physical level as well, by curing an incurable disease.
A. Smith – teacher/Singer/ artist

Dear Rose, I came across your work, initially on the internet, YouTube videos with interest. I browsed your website. Your work is much needed in today's SUFFERING world. Your journey through life with challenging experiences that you have sought to heal from & Share with the world is an example to us all. Can you please send me a copy of "The Book Without a Name". I enclose $40.00 with warm Regard -Tracey from U.K.

Hell! Where were you all my life Ms. Rose!
We need more **authentic teachers'** like you!
I LOVE YOU! From-Canada- Majer

This is an easy to read journey that challenges us to think and grow outside of our comfort zone. We shouldn't believe what others dictate to us out of manipulation. We must trust our true inner spirit. I appreciate Rose sharing her experience so that others may learn, heal and grow in wisdom.   Blessing Divine Soul, from S. C. –Luke

Ms. Rose, Thank you for writing an inspiring, healing and empowering book. I was contemplating suicide until a friend gave me your book as a gift and I read it. –Alicia - N. Y.

Hi Rose, thank you so much for the inspiration...from talking to you at the Brooklyn book fair and reading your book. I was very touched. I was crying in the pages when you wrote about your father and godmother. And I admired your gentle heart upon the death of frank. God bless you, you are a bunch of love. You don't know how much healing you have begun in my own hurting soul. It takes a really honest and powerful writer to bring me, another writer to tears and reflection. Thank you so much from the bottom of my heart. 9-25-13 -   Love M. from the Philippians

THANK YOU ROSE!
I am older than you in age and have learned (like you say remember) my GODDESS SELF and inner and over-standing UNIVERSEAL LAWS and APPLYING the WISDOW, I healed my body and LIVING (not EXISTING anymore NOW LIVIING A JOYOUS LIFE! Love always,   - BRAZIL A. Cruz

THANK PRECIOUS ONE!
AS MAN THAT IS HARD HEADED, READING YOUR BOOKS WAS BETTER THAN GOING TO A PSYCHAITRIST. THIS WAS MY BEST DIVINE THERAPY SESSION, WE ARE BLESSED YOU ARE HERE. –LOVE JUAN from D.R.

Hello,
I'm from Guadeloupe, an island in the Caribbean. I discovered your youtube channel while looking for videos with Black Dot. I almost immediately found your youtube channel with the 2 extracts you have with him. I was so impressed by it and learned so much from it that I then decided to watch each one of the excerpt of your TV program. After, I bought your first book. Today I have finished my second reading. I have already

bought your second book and I will start reading it. Of course, I also plan after it to buy and read the third one. I'm writing you because I wanted to thank you for what you do. I have learned a lot and also grow a lot from your program excerpts. Also, there are many things that happened in my life I simply couldn't understand and thanks to what you do I can now understand them and as I previously said grow from them. My dearest will is to keep on growing spiritually and there are now choices I can make clearly because I see things more clearly about who we (humans) are.

I loved your book 'The Book without a Name.'
1. Nice and short
2. I liked the bold print, but found parts hard on my eyes as the print size changes for example page 104-105
3. Couldn't over stand your thoughts on the creator/religion/bible. You are not in to church etc. I do know your belief in the creator. The bible has had a lot of faults yet you place a lot of the bible scriptures into your book although they were of benefit to me.
I look forward to reading your other works. One very important thing I should mention is I am still working on things from your book that is truly helping me.
Blessings always!   Jane S.

Hi! TRUE DIVINE ONE! I watched your video clips on youtube and I was very impressed with your divine messages, your courage and integrity to do the Creator WILL! You come from your heart not the false EGO for FAME and GREED. I read your 3 books and can't wait for

the next book it helped me on all levels of my life. I am learning as you said (REMEMBERING) how to love, forgive myself and others and to trust my higher self. I inner and overstand now as a male I need to TRULY HUMBLE MYSELF to PRIME CREATOR/ GOD. LOVE YOU!!!!!
-G. V. from Sedona, Arizona

DEAR Ms. ROSE, I THANK YOU FOR WRITING SUCH POWERFUL HEALING BOOKS, I PRAYED FOR A TRUE SPIRITUAL TEACHER, MOVED IN THE BLOCK 2015 NOT KNOWING UNTIL 3 MONTHS LATER THAT YOU LIVE DIRECTLY ACROSS THE STREET. —B. Glover - Bx. N.Y.

YOU ARE THE DIVINE ONE!!! OWN YOU DIVINE POWER NOW!!! R. W.

THANK YOU ALL FOR YOUR LOVE OFFERING (ENERGY EXCHANGE) DONATIONS.

ROSE'S NEWEST TWO BOOKS ENTITED: ASCENSION, SOUL RETRIEVAL, RESURRECTION part #1 and part #2 - ARE AVAILABLE NOW. And HER NEXT BOOK ENTITLED: "WHY? WIL BE RELEASE THE END OF 2015

IF YOU ARE READY HER BOOKS WILL HELP EXPAND YOUR CONSCIOUSNESS EVEN MORE TO RECONNECT TO YOUR DIVINE POWER WITHIN. YOU WILL CHANGE YOUR LIFE FOREVER!

Made in the USA
Middletown, DE
19 September 2015